THE
LEGACY
OF THE
BUTTERFLIES

THE STORY OF THE BRAVE SISTERS WHO TOPPLED A
DICTATOR AND CHANGED THE COURSE OF A NATION

D1707794

ZOE MARQUETTI

ISBN: 9798422992676

Cover Design by: C5 Designs

DEDICATION

To my mother - for your infinite love and strength. You were my butterfly.

PREFACE

On November 25th 1960, the three Mirabal sisters Patria, Minerva, and Maria Teresa, were brutally clubbed to death and strangled in a corn field, along with their driver, Rufino de la Cruz. The shocking incident led to the overthrow of the ruthless dictator Rafael Leónidas Trujillo Molina, who had ruled the Dominican Republic for over 30 years with an iron fist.

The three sisters, known as Las Mariposas, became symbols of popular and feminine resistance. A fourth sister, Dedé, was left behind to raise their children and she dedicated her life to preserving her sisters' legacy until her own death in 2014.

In 1999, the United Nations General Assembly designated November 25th as the International Day for the Elimination of Violence Against Women in honor of the Mirabal sisters.

This is their story.

"What matters is the quality of a person.
What someone is inside themselves"
— Maria Teresa Mirabal

TABLE OF CONTENTS

INTRODUCTION

The abuse of power is as old as time itself.

Since we started learning of Greek mythology, we have heard tales of gods like Zeus abducting and raping many women at will, including his own daughters. Throughout the centuries, history has shown us that reality is really no different, with those enjoying a self-imposed god-like status using their positions of power to exploit women whenever they felt like it. It's a phenomenon that we still witness today, with the #MeToo movement exposing many examples of sexual abuse and harassment by prominent figures.

In every case that we come across, the perpetrator takes on a particular role, be that of patriarch, political leader, priest, protector, or mentor. What they all have in common is a love of power and the accompanying hubris to exert their will on the powerless. And a person who believes they can have it all doesn't handle rejection too well.

More often than not, such figures confuse the position of status they are holding with their own personal ambitions, seeing themselves *as* 'the power' rather than the mechanism by which the position itself can function. This provides them with the validation they need to do whatever they desire without consequences or fear of backlash. It matters not if you are talking about a movie mogul or a head of state; each player believes themself to be untouchable and above the law.

1

Women have also been known to use power to their advantage but more often than not, adopt the role of facilitators for their influential husbands or partners. While dictators commit blatant acts of brutality, society too often silently participates by turning a blind eye to such actions. When such a man becomes 'the power', he is able to control those around him, his environment, and the wider establishment either through intimidation, ingratiation, violence, or worse.

More than 60 years ago, three of the four sisters were brutally murdered for standing up against one man and his reign of terror. Although it wouldn't be the first time that women have fallen victim to systemic violence exercised by powerful regimes, the event paved the way for a newer, brighter future. The story of the Mirabal sisters is just one example out of millions where the abuse of power and authoritarianism is finally brought down by those with very little real 'power'... the butterflies.

The setting is the Dominican Republic: a small island in the Caribbean, then ruled by the dictator Rafael Leónidas Trujillo Molina. Also known as 'El Jefe' (The Boss), he held power from 1930 until his assassination in 1961. The victims: three sisters from a middle class family who were secretly working with an underground movement to bring down the ruthless oppressor and establish democracy in their country.

The story follows a well-scripted scenario: a powerful man turns his attention to a beautiful young girl, Minerva Mirabal. When he is rebuffed, his fragile ego is sorely damaged, with devastating consequences. Not only does he refuse to grant her a license to practice as a lawyer on her graduation from university, but he also targets her family throughout his reign of terror. As the sisters become more politicized, their involvement in clandestine operations to bring down Trujillo comes to his attention.

He strikes the final blow, by having all three sisters and their driver brutally beaten to death and their car pushed over a cliff to make it look like an accident. This was the beginning of the end for Trujillo, having gone too far in the eyes of the downtrodden people of the Dominican Republic and its international backers. He was himself gunned down by CIA-sponsored conspirators in 1961, bringing to an end one of the most brutal regimes in the whole of the Caribbean Basin and Latin America of that period.

But what is interesting about this story is the fact that it wasn't the political activities of the Mirabal sisters that initially caught his attention. It was his lecherous desire to have any young girl he wanted, in this case, Minerva Mirabal. When she refused his advances at a formal party organized with the intention of gathering young, fresh-faced, middle-class women together for his amusement, he was furious. To add insult to injury, her family left the party before him, resulting in a torrent of rage that was to follow them for years.

No one says no to a dictator – that's rule number one of the dictator's handbook. To be a good dictator, you have to be a very special person, at least in your own eyes. Trujillo certainly fit this description and displayed many signs of classic dictator psychology. He demanded admiration and had little sympathy for those who weren't willing to give it. His grandiose ego made him want to be the center of attention and his narcissist tendencies could very easily be slighted by anyone going against his will.

By its very nature, dictatorship entails control, intimidation, influence, fear, and violence. Trujillo was a master at each one, which is exactly why he managed to stay in power for so long. You only have to recall names such as Adolf Hitler, Josef Stalin, Benito Mussolini, Pol Pot or Idi Amin from recent history to understand how a dictator thinks and works. Just like all of the aforementioned, Trujillo was bent on maintaining complete control over every aspect of public and private life, using terror, torture, and intimidation to do so. But it is his personal sexual whims and fetishes that added to his notoriety, because they were no secret.

Trujillo brazenly demanded to have unmarried girls in his bed and would wreak revenge on any family that refused to give up their daughters. His predatory sexual desires were so interwoven with his political persona that he was seen by many as more of a monster than a man. And yet, he had the Church and Establishment on his side for quite a long time, which allowed him to do whatever he liked, and he usually did.

Dictators like Trujillo have another thing in common: they suffer from extreme anxiety, mostly related to paranoid fears of civil uprisings and/or assassination. It is almost as if the more powerful they become, the more vulnerable they feel. When the woman who has rejected your sexual advances is now conspiring to remove you from power behind your back, that's a situation any narcissist would find unbearable. In addition to that, fear of 'the enemy', be that communism or any idea that threatens your position, leads to greater silencing of any voice of resistance.

Despite living in fear, the sisters and their husbands continued to work clandestinely toward bringing an end to the notorious Trujillo regime. They were fanned by a profound desire for social justice and encouraged by recent events in nearby Cuba, where the revolutionary Fidel Castro had just come to power (little did they know that Castro was a wolf in a sheep's clothing). They continued to live regular family lives, raising children, and working on their farm, despite several periods of incarceration and continued uncertainty.

Minerva could not have known back at that infamous party that her actions would eventually lead to the death of her father or the imprisonment of her husband and brothers-in-law. Neither could she have envisaged that neither she nor her sisters would ever see their children again after the women were savagely murdered on the way back from a prison visit.

The Mirabals certainly wouldn't have imagined that their deaths would spark international outrage and be instrumental in the ultimate downfall of the Trujillo regime. The butterflies, as they were widely known, became synonymous with hope and freedom for those opposing the dictatorship in the Dominican Republic. Their legacy of resistance means that they remain symbols of bravery and courage throughout the world to this day.

But let's start at the beginning, in a lush Caribbean land first named Hispaniola by Christopher Columbus in 1492. A land which later became a hotbed of civil turmoil, foreign intervention and political chaos.

Welcome to the Dominican Republic of 1930.

CHAPTER 1
HURRICANES AND HEROES

"The people have always some champion whom they set over them and nurse into greatness.... This and no other is the root from which a tyrant springs; when he first appears he is a protector."
—Plato

One of the biggest hurricanes ever recorded and the fifth deadliest in the Atlantic hit the Dominican Republic in 1930. Hurricane San Zenón was the second of three tropical cyclones of the season, first observed in the Lesser Antilles before moving to a Category 4 hurricane. As it passed over the Dominican Republic, it completely ravaged the island, killing as many as 8,000 people in the area. This natural disaster paved the way for the rise of the New Patria and the dictatorship of Trujillo.

The hurricane, which struck the island on September 2 and 3 in 1930, destroyed the nation's capital of Santo Domingo, wrecked the local infrastructure, and caused hundreds to perish. Torrential rain brought severe flooding, wiping out the port facilities, customs houses, bridges, and riverbank settlements. Winds of up to 150 miles per hour flattened the tin-roofed, wooden buildings that had been built during the rapid urbanization from 1916 onwards, leaving survivors to rummage through the rubble for their deceased family members.

With the death toll reaching an unprecedented scale, homelessness and hunger were to follow, creating the perfect opportunity for the new leader

General Rafael Leónidas Trujillo to step in. After having facilitated the overthrow of the government of President Horacio Vásquez on February 23rd, 1930 in a coup d'état, he set about organizing the relief effort with great military tact, using the cyclone as a key trope to legitimize his rule. The destruction caused by the hurricane allowed Trujillo to capitalize on his totalitarian plans to become a national savior and construct a New Homeland, or Nueva Patria.

He wrote; *"I had scarcely begun to undertake this staggering program when—sixteen days after my inauguration—a tremendous cataclysm destroyed the nation's capital. The San Zenón Hurricane, as it came to be known, left thousands of victims, a wrecked city, and a grisly panorama of death and desolation. The tragedy had the effect of precipitating my plans. It created sadly propitious circumstances for their implementation. I could exercise my capacity for organization and leadership, which had been developed during my military career. I was able with this demonstration to restore some degree of confidence, which was the foundation of the moral reconstruction I proposed."*

The natural disaster allowed Trujillo to demonstrate his leadership abilities, to later implement his totalitarian policies, and act as a platform for the creation of a new national psychology of solidarity under his wing. His actions were, in fact, to tear the country apart.

A peaceful land

The Dominican Republic had seen many troubles in its turbulent history, ever since Columbus first set foot on the island in 1492. Storms of all sorts; political, social, and economic, wreaked havoc on the island over the centuries, with the population suffering great losses as a result. On Columbus' arrival, he initially found the Taino living there. These were indigenous people of the Arawak Caribbeans who inhabited most of what we now know as Cuba, Jamaica, Puerto Rico, and the Lesser Antilles. They called the eastern part of their home *Quisqueya*, meaning 'mother of all lands', and the western side was known as *Ayiti* (land of high mountains), from where Haiti takes its name.

These people lived in a well-organized, religious society and were self-sufficient, being skilled in agriculture, fishing, and hunting. Each community was led by a chief and they mostly enjoyed a peaceful existence working the land, creating beautifully sculpted pottery, and taking part in religious ceremonies and customs. Columbus was struck by the friendliness of these natives and immediately saw their usefulness, writing in his journals, *"They were very well built, with very handsome bodies and very good faces....They do not carry arms or know them....They should be good servants."*

Claiming the island for the Spanish Crown, Columbus renamed it La Isla Española ('The Spanish Island'), later Latinized to Hispaniola. During the late fifteenth and early sixteenth centuries, the Spanish subsequently conquered the island, enslaving its inhabitants and forcing them off their land to work in gold mines and colonial plantations. Diseases brought by the Spanish such as smallpox and rising starvation due to lack of cultivated crops led to high mortality rates of the indigenous population, killing almost 90% of the surviving Taino by 1519. It's estimated that almost 3 million Taino souls had died by then, almost wiping the indigenous population off the face of the earth.

Many Conquistadors took Taino women as wives, and the importation of African slaves also formed a population with Creole characteristics. They were subjects of the Spanish colonies and lived in what became known as the Spanish Captaincy General of Santo Domingo until 1821. Needless to say, Hispaniola suffered terribly at the hands of the New World order, in which a cruel, exploitative, slave-based society and economy came into being. Churches, monasteries, and hospitals were established on the island, as well as the first university in 1538, although a strict class and caste system were in place, which the Catholic Church cruelly enforced.

Although Hispaniola's gold mines and lush plantations yielded great wealth in the first 500 years of Spanish rule, the gradual decimation of the indigenous 'working' population led the Spanish to look further afield for more lucrative conquests. Those who were ambitious enough moved to Peru and Mexico, leaving Hispaniola totally neglected for the next three centuries. It lay vulnerable to raids by British, Dutch, and French marauders, who set about to completely ransack the island over this period. In 1795, the western part of it was eventually ceded to the French and renamed Saint-Domingue (which was later to become Haiti).

Rebellion and uprisings
The island enjoyed a period of relative prosperity as a sugar-producing colony supported by slavery and saw a mild economic boom in the 18th century until a slave uprising occurred.

Fueled by the desire for freedom of political rights and more humane conditions for the black slaves, the Haitians managed to overthrow the French under the leadership of Toussaint-Louverture. The rebels overran parts of the eastern island too, instilling terror in the ruling white class until they were driven back by Dominican colonists and British forces. In 1809, the colony was reunited with Spain but the Spanish governor was deposed in 1821 by a group of Dominicans and declared independent. The fledgling nation was now named the Independent State of Spanish Haiti.

It wasn't long before trouble arose again, this time with the Haitian troops led by Jean-Pierre Boyer (president of Haiti, 1818-43) overrunning the eastern part of the island and occupying it from 1822 to 1842. During that period, the Haitians took control of the government, severed the church's ties with Rome, forced out the traditional ruling class, and almost obliterated the western European and Hispanic traditions. Despite ethnic tensions and a lot of barbarity, the slaves were emancipated and the administration ran rather smoothly during this period.

When a devastating earthquake took place in 1842, the 'Father of Independence', Juan Pablo Duarte, organized a secret society to fight the Haitians. The outbreak of civil war in Haiti itself eventually led to independence being achieved in 1844 although Duarte and other freedom fighters were forced into exile. After that, several military strongmen (caudillos) played for power in the Dominican Republic, with dictatorial presidents consistently selling out the country to foreign and commercial interests. Misadministration and overspending bankrupted the government in 1861, with Spain stepping in again to reclaim its former colony. In 1865, the Spanish withdrew once more to leave the islanders fighting amongst themselves.

Instability and salvation
The instability continued during the 1870s until an idealist reformer called Ulises Espaillat was elected president, establishing the first democratic government on the island. Unfortunately, his success was short-lived as he was overthrown in 1876, with civil unrest ensuing until the emergence of Ulises Heureaux. During his presidency, from 1882 to 1899, new roads and irrigation canals were built, foreign investment flooded in and agriculture production increased. Like his predecessors though, Heureaux ruled with a dictatorial hand, engaging a secret police force and taking control of the press, as well as committing electoral fraud.

He was assassinated by his rival, Ramón Cáceres, in 1899 and the country spiraled into the chaos of the past, with new leaders taking over and then

11

being ousted in the years to come. Even the archbishop, Adolfo Nouel, took on the presidency in 1912 but failed to restore order and was forced to resign four months later. An interest in the Dominican Republic then came from an unlikely source; the United States, which was now a major trading partner in the Caribbean and recognized Hispaniola's strategic position on a major sea route.

In 1905, the United States took over the administration of the country's customs agency to pay off its European creditors, going on to assume complete control of the nation's government in 1916. Thousands of troops were placed in the Dominican Republic and neighboring Haiti, which the US also administered from 1915 to 1934. During this time, roads, schools, and sanitation facilities were built, with legal reforms being put in place to allow US-owned sugarcane companies to expand.

The islanders were introduced to chewing gum and baseball and when the US military departed, they left behind a modern military police force that became instrumental in future power grabs. The Dominicans deeply resented their loss of sovereignty and reforms brought in by the US that had dispossessed thousands of peasants, leaving them without legal claim to their own lands.

Tyranny and power
When Horacio Vásquez came to head the government in 1924, backed by the U.S., he proved to be incompetent and corrupt. His removal from power came during a revolution that was also partly triggered by the knock-on effect of the Great Depression and the slump in the sugar market. The armed forces were led at the time by one General Rafael Trujillo, who ordered his troops to remain in their barracks and allowed the revolution to take place before seizing power himself. Thus began the 'Era of Trujillo'; one of the longest, cruelest, and most absolute dictatorships in modern history.

The Dominican people were now forced to endure a totalitarian regime that lasted for thirty-one years, during which time, the personal desires of the dictator were completely fused with those of the Dominican state itself. Never before in the history of Latin America had a single ruler imposed such widespread control and coercion over the minds and lives of his people.

Society and its norms

This dark period of tyranny was only just beginning when three-year-old Minerva Mirabal was growing up on her father's farm in the small village of Ojo de Agua in Salcedo Province in 1930. She and her sisters were removed from the harsh realities of Trujillo's regime during their younger years, immersed in the bucolic life organized around the farm, a coffee mill, and a general store.

The Dominicans had known civil wars and revolutions, with governments coming and going. They had seen regional caudillos taking power; peasant farmers who often rose to high ranks, making socio-political mobility a familiar phenomenon. It was, therefore, no surprise that someone like Trujillo should come from such humble beginnings. With most of the population illiterate in the early part of the 20th century, positions of power were often occupied by those with little schooling.

During the U.S. occupation, some reforms were put in place that allowed women to study writing and shorthand so they could enter the civil service, with several of them going on to take up jobs within the government. In the decades that followed, education improved across the country and women began to pursue careers in medicine and in other professions popular at the time. El Jefe assumed control of who was appointed in which job within the government and many private industries also came under his jurisdiction.

Nonetheless, a national middle-class had emerged that combined the older bourgeoisie with new entrepreneurs and a large amalgamated commercial/industrial/agricultural/professional class came into being that interacted via sporting events and social clubs. At the same time, Trujillo could relate with those respectable Dons from small towns or rural regions who had some education and standing. These families still had influence in the local scene and belonged to the 'old' bourgeoisie who owned land, domestic servants, had access to education and were aware of the growing abuse of power at the top.

It's within this climate that Trujillo established his presidency, keen to make sure that everyone was at his disposal. The society was already patriarchal and it was easy for him to fit into that role, which also suited his machismo tendencies. The death of the Mirabal sisters is often viewed as the factor which eventually toppled him from power, although his reasons for murdering them weren't only political. The act also tied in with his feelings about the role of women, or rather his lack of feelings for them. He objectified even his wives as a means to achieve his ambitions and often took multiple mistresses, exhibiting a great sense of entitlement in doing so.

The Mirabal sisters contradicted traditional gender roles and had been brought up to speak their minds. When dictatorship emerged in their country, this was a dangerous privilege. While their husbands were probably more politically active, they were subsequently released from detainment, while the women were targeted. No doubt, their activities represented a shift in gender norms as they defiantly resisted the patriarchy, hurting Trujillo's pride at the same time.

But who was Trujillo really? Where did he come from and how was he able to keep a stranglehold on a country for over 30 years? In the next chapter, we will take a look at the man behind one of the most brutal regimes of the 20th century.

CHAPTER 2
A BEAST OF MANY NAMES

"Dictators ride to and fro upon tigers which they dare not dismount.
And the tigers are getting hungry."
—Winston Churchill

Often, the way a man dies reflects the way he lived his life. When the dictator Trujillo was gunned down by his assailants on the street, they were later hailed as national heroes.

The cruelest tyrant in Latin America left the capital in his chauffeur-driven Chevrolet Bel Air on the night of May 30 1961 to meet up with one of his mistresses. A team of 14 assassins laid in wait for him, determined to bring to an end the dark shadow of terror that had hung over the Dominican Republic for thirty years.

While most of the plotters were rounded up and killed by Trujillo's son in the days that followed the assassination, one of the drivers managed to find refuge in the Italian Embassy. Major General Antonio Imbert Barrera was given the military title in gratitude for his role in Trujillo's death and despite fearing recriminations by supporters of the dictator for the remainder of his life, he had no regrets about his actions.

Such was the hatred for Trujillo that anyone instrumental in bringing him down was seen as a hero, and Imbert himself certainly never regretted his actions. In an interview he gave to the BBC in 2011, before his own death in 2016, he was asked if he was happy to have shot the Dominican dictator all those years ago, *"Sure,"* he replied. *"Nobody told me to go and kill Trujillo. The only way to get rid of him was to kill him."*

A leader who has nurtured so much hatred amongst his people is never mourned, although it takes a lot of guts to risk one's life to try to take him out. And when that leader portrays himself as a national savior helped by a secret police that commits acts of unthinkable barbarity, it's not difficult to imagine that his persona strikes terror in the hearts of all under his rule.

But what do we know of this tyrant and how did he manage to exert absolute control over the Dominican Republic for so many decades?

The white-faced mulatto
Rafael Leónidas Trujillo was born on October 24, 1891 in San Cristobal, a poor village on the south coast of the Dominican Republic. He was the third of 11 children in a working-class family of Spanish, Dominican, and Haitian descent. Despite his great-grandmother coming from the Haitian mulatto (mixed race) class, his later biography obscured this aspect of his family history and many of the true facts surrounding his life remain uncertain to this day.

Rather than admitting to his Haitian heritage, he claimed to be of noble descent, his forebears supposedly including a Spanish army officer and a French marquis. After rising to power, he must have always been conscious of his mulatto background, and was said to wear make-up to give the appearance of his skin being lighter than it actually was. Needless to say, anyone pointing to his black heritage was said to be committing an act of treason.

16

What we do know is that he received a very rudimentary education and by the time he was 16, had taken on the job of telegraph operator. He soon became involved in petty crime though, forming a street gang, and losing his job when he was arrested for forging a check. His criminal record was later conveniently destroyed when a fire in the Dominican Republic Supreme Court Buildings in 1927 burnt all documents.

The family man

He got married in 1916 to Aminta Ledesima and subsequently had two daughters. At this point, he needed to find secure employment and managed to do so by becoming a private security guard at a sugar plantation. His first taste of power must have excited his megalomaniacal tendencies

When the American occupation of the Dominican Republic began in 1914 following 50 years of revolution after revolution, one of the first things the occupying forces did was to establish a Dominican police force. This must have sounded right down Trujillo's street, and in 1918 he signed up as a cadet, training with the US marines as a member of the National Guard. His ascent within the military ranks was meteoric and he impressed his superiors with his natural leadership qualities. After graduating from the Haina Military Academy in 1921, he assumed the rank of Lieutenant Colonel in 1924 before being promoted to Brigadier General in 1927. A year later, he would have full control of the Dominican Army.

The rise of a tyrant

It wasn't long before Trujillo found the chance to seize absolute power when President Horacio Vásquez was opposed by revolutionaries in 1930. Although declaring his neutrality, Trujillo had a secret agenda, maneuvering himself into the presidential seat when Vásquez was forced to resign. Being the only candidate in the presidential election, he secured 95 percent of the vote with the help of intimidation and violence. Not long after that, Hurricane San Zenón hit the island, devastating the population and infrastructure. There could have been no greater opportunity for him to show off his organizational prowess while announcing a state of emergency and martial law, as well as establishing a tight grip on the economy. The stage was set for the rise of a tyrant.

His legacy of autocratic rule involved silencing his enemies and eliminating his opponents. His political adversaries seemed to 'disappear', with strange car crashes, accidental suicides, arrests, and executions becoming part of the daily news feed. The right to assembly was denied, freedom of the press became non-existent, and independent trade unions were abolished. The rights of all citizens were replaced by blackmail, bribery, and terror.

The one-party state asked government employees to 'donate' 10 percent of their salaries to the national treasury and those who did not join the party risked imprisonment. He took ownership of all the national assets, including the airlines, trading monopolies, manufacturers, and most sugarcane plantations, possessing as much as three-fifths of the nation's gross domestic product and workforce.

A rebuilt capital was now named Ciudad Trujillo (Trujillo City) in his honor and many streets, monuments, and landmarks bore his name too. Every home was to have a picture of Trujillo gracing their walls and the slogan, 'In this home, Trujillo is boss' became ingrained in the public psyche. This was further instilled by car license plates bearing the words Viva Trujillo! and churches were required to post the slogan 'Dios en Cielo, Trujillo en Tierra' - God in Heaven, Trujillo on Earth. He even named a mountain after himself and every town or sporting event had to be dedicated to the 'Benefactor of the Fatherland' and 'Father of the New Fatherland'. Other honorary titles he bestowed upon himself were 'Rebuilder of the Financial Independence of the Republic', 'First Journalist', 'Chief Protector of the Dominican Working Class', and 'Genius of the Peace'. Clearly, his ego knew no bounds.

Trujillo was also keen to turn the Dominican Republic into a modern, white, country, despite his Haitian roots, and he used women's public presence in order to do so. As he controlled the media and public life, he began to try to change the perception of the country by enlisting his fair-skinned daughters and other public female figures such as actress Maria Montez to do so. He staged grand events aimed at reframing the nation in terms of race, attempting to create an image of the Dominican people as light-skinned mestizos. Annual beauty pageants appointed young, upper-class women as queens and princesses and in the lavish Free World's Fair of Peace and Confraternity organized in 1955, his daughter Angelita was even crowned 'Queen Angelita the First'!

The hungry tiger
It's not unusual for tyrants to personify themselves as god-like figures and along with that comes a belief that they can do whatever they like. Trujillo became known for his insatiable sexual appetite, despite being married, and took many mistresses over the years. He was most reviled for his habit of seizing young women and raping them at will, something that he apparently did on a massive scale. His appetite for young virgins was so well-known that families used to hide their daughters when he was visiting their areas. If he took a fancy to one, the family could not refuse him so his presence incited fear and intimidation.

Trujillo was a man who had a lot to live up to. He had come from humble origins and was by no means a member of the upper class. But his sexual bravado was accepted as it fit in with the societal norms of machismo behavior, with the traditional aggrandizement of how many women a man could lay.

Wanting to work his way up through the social strata, he selected women of superior status, marrying Bienvenida Ricardo Martínez in 1927. A year later he began an affair with María de los Angeles Martínez Alba and after divorcing Bienvenida in 1935, he married Martínez. He had a daughter with Bienvenida, three children with María Martínez, and two more with Lina Lovatón Pittaluga, who he met in 1937.

He earned the reputation of being 'the big man' – the caudillo-turned-statesman who portrayed the man as head of the family – one that could often be violent and dominant. While promoting the image of father and defender of the extended family, he also enjoyed being seen as a great lover. Acquiring women through sexual conquest brought him even greater social status and a blind eye was turned by his peers to the abduction of young girls for his sexual pleasure.

He was the tiger; the epitome of the popular underdog who gained power and prestige through accomplishing great things. His vanity demanded that he always be impeccably dressed, while he was seen by many as charming, daring, and audacious. At the same time, he was, in effect, humiliating the elite by seeking out their daughters, as well as placing himself within their circles. If there was anything that could earn you respect, it was prestige, and he saw his conquests as ratifying his position, often at the annoyance of those paying lip service to him.

In his well-known book entitled, Trujillo: Little Caesar of the Caribbean (1956), the Dominican journalist and exile Germán E. Ornes wrote, *"Being too busy to court beautiful girls himself, Trujillo has special aides charged with that chore. The years pass but the fires of passion are not smothered in Trujillo's heart, so even to this day many Dominicans, including fathers and brothers, make their good fortunes over the virtue of a beautiful and willing female relative or friend. Notwithstanding rumors to the contrary, other men's wives are not in demand, since Trujillo likes to hold exclusive rights upon his women. His favorites and former girlfriends are all 'marked women' and no man can get close to them without risk."*

Clearly, women were often exploited by family members in order to gain favor from Trujillo, which meant that he had an unwavering supply of fresh victims to exploit. Although it's hard to know exactly how many women suffered directly at his hands, we can assume that it was enough to satisfy his lustful appetite and maintain the climate of fear.

Attack on the nation

While Trujillo went around promoting family values and morality, he was behaving in exactly the opposite way. The eventual murder of the Mirabal sisters showed a deep disrespect for the sanctity of the home, which embodied women in the role of mothers and family-makers. It was actually an attack on national morality, which explains why the event was the last straw for the public at large.

Many other women were also politically active in the Dominican Republic in the 1940s and 50s and the Mirabal sisters were not unique in that. The female population was growing increasingly outraged at the number of broken homes and orphans created by the dictator's policy of murdering male political opponents or their incarceration for long periods of time. Those who spoke out against the government lost their jobs and livelihood, as did their family members, which caused severe hardship for many.

Without realizing it, Trujillo was encouraging more women to be politically active because of his heavy-handedness; they were experiencing the abuse of the regime at close range. Rather than preserving the mother-centric rhetoric that is a tactic widely used in Latin America, such as in Nicaragua and Chile, he was actually destroying it. While encouraging women to fulfill stereotypical roles as mothers and carers, he was forcing them to rebel against a system that was attacking those very family values. By violating the purity of the home, abducting young daughters and tearing families apart, he was shaping his own downfall.

The policies of violence

The tyrannical president did nothing to improve his reputation when he ordered the massacre of 10,000 to 25,000 Haitians in 1937, although the event went scarcely unnoticed in the international press. Many of the victims were economic migrants working on the sugar plantations and squatting on the Haiti-Dominican Republic border while others had been born in the Dominican Republic. They were accused of stealing cattle and crops from local residents, which was purely an excuse for Trujillo to wipe them out. He commanded his army to kill all Haitians living on the northwestern frontier and the Cibao region and they proceeded to do so over a six-day period.

The Haitians were savagely murdered with rifles, machetes, shovels, knives, and bayonets and included women and children. Survivors told of family members being hacked to death with machetes or strangled, and of children being bashed against rocks and tree trunks. Obsessed with 'whitening' the nation, the dictator (of Haitian descent himself) was a strong proponent of ethnic cleansing, He saw the Haitians as racially and culturally inferior, being of African race and not useful to the social and economic development of the country.

He pandered to a rising trend coming from Europe, influenced by the Nazi policies of Aryanism, and described Haitians as, "...*frankly undesirable. Of pure African race, they cannot represent for us any ethnic incentive. Not well nourished and worse dressed, they are weak, though very prolific due to their low living conditions. For that same reason, the Haitian that enters lives afflicted by numerous and capital vices and is necessarily affected by diseases and physiological deficiencies which are endemic at the lowest levels of that society.*"

The event became known as the Parsley Massacre, because soldiers asked dark-skinned people to say the word "perejil", which is Spanish for parsley, in order to determine who was Haitian. For the Creole-speaking people, the 'r' was difficult to pronounce and those who couldn't say the word properly met with a violent death. The massacre fell within the new policy that Trujillo called the 'Dominicanisation of the frontier' and not long after, he set about changing place names along the border from Creole and French to Spanish. Quotas were imposed on how many foreign workers companies could hire, and Haitians were prevented from remaining after the sugar harvest was over.

Controversy seemed to shadow the dictator as the decades passed by, with his barbaric reputation coupled with his greed for greater and greater wealth. Some of his actions were also quite brazen and included the murder of exiled opponent Jesús María de Galíndez in New York in 1956, as well as an attempt to assassinate Venezuelan president Rómulo Betancourt with a car bomb in 1960. His reign of terror at home was carried out by the Military Intelligence Agency who expedited horrendous acts on Trujillo's behalf. In one incident on June 14, 1959, leftist Dominican exiles planning to invade the Dominican Republic from Cuba were captured and 217 were killed. Some of them met gruesome deaths by being pushed out of a Dominican Air Force plane in mid-air.

Nepotism and political puppetry allowed Trujillo to remain highly influential, even when there was a backlash against him after the Haitian massacre. Jacinto Peynado became president of the Dominican Republic from 1938 to 1940, with Trujillo holding firmly onto the reins and continuing to control almost every aspect of government and politics. In 1940, Manuel de Jesus Troncoso de la Concha became president and, in effect, he took a double oath to follow both the Constitution and Trujillo. El Jefe returned to power in 1942 and 1952 until his brother Hector took over, keeping the grip over the country a family affair. Trujillo himself was appointed as Commander in Chief of the armed forces.

A man of many names and personas, Trujillo managed to create such a strong personality cult that many people found it difficult to believe he had actually died. His omnipresence had pervaded all aspects of Dominican life, from Generalisimo to Benefactor of the Fatherland. His Napoleonic appearances at state functions of medal-bedecked military costumes and plumed chapeau made him appear invincible. But he wasn't.

Although Trujillo preferred to be known as El Jefe (The Boss), most Dominicans remember him as El Chivo (The Goat). The moniker was first used by the underground resistance as a kind of code name when planning his assassination and a song was even written after the event to celebrate his downfall. Bandleader Antonio Morel released a merengue (the national music of the Dominican Republic) called 'Mataron al Chivo' (They killed the goat) to celebrate his death and it is a song still sung to this day.

Chapter 3
Blood Ties

"When injustice becomes law, rebellion becomes duty."
—*Minerva Mirabal*

Why would three middle-class women with children get involved in a plot to overthrow a president? Where did they find the courage to stand up to one of the most evil tyrants in modern history? To understand that, we have to look at the times the Mirabal family were living in.

When Trujillo came to power in 1930, he undertook the restoration of a country devastated by a hurricane. Regardless of his clampdown on freedom and stranglehold on the public sphere, there's no denying that he must have brought a sense of hope and salvation to a people living in a largely rural, underdeveloped society. His promises to bring the country into the 20th century were kept to a certain extent, and the quality of life improved in general. Poverty still existed but he managed to expand the economy and wipe out most of the national debt during his reign.

There was an expansion of the middle class during the relatively stable economic climate that prevailed. The road system was enhanced, port facilities were improved, public buildings and airports were constructed, and illiteracy fell as the public education system grew. To a society that had never experienced such advancements, it must have seemed like they were finally catching up with the modern world. Despite Trujillo's extremist tactics to suppress the opposition and his nepotistic control of the nation's wealth, many people benefited from his policies throughout the years.

Not having any other kind of stable government to compare to, it's understandable that many Dominicans were impressed with their president's actions, at least regarding the improved standards of living. Observers of that era even suggest that if Trujillo had put himself forward in a democratic election, it's quite possible that he would have won a majority of the popular vote right up until the final years of his dictatorship.

Growing up under tyranny

It was around this time that the Mirabal sisters were born, growing up in a society that was trying to maintain economic stability while suffering from political tyranny. Enrique Mirabal Fernández, a successful farmer and merchant, was the father of the Mirabal sisters. He married Mercedes "Chea" Reyes Camilo in 1923, who was also from a middle-class family. They owned and ran a successful farm, coffee mill, and rice factory, as well as a shop and meat market in the village of Ojo de Agua, near Salcedo.

Although successful landowners, it's believed that the family had no sympathies for Trujillo and didn't have his portrait hanging proudly on the walls of their home, which was an act of revolt in itself. Despite that, no one openly criticized the government if they knew what was good for them, as the secret police had eyes and ears in every town and village in the country. In addition, the government had appropriated many of the nation's assets and land, enforcing monopolies on products such as rice, salt, and meat, meaning that the landowners were always fearful of having their property seized on the whim of the president.

The girls were raised in their family home, just 67 miles (108 km) northwest of the capital of Santo Domingo, and probably enjoyed a relatively peaceful upbringing that wasn't dominated by politics per se.

It is perhaps due to their mother, Mercedes, that they were encouraged to receive a good education. Being illiterate herself, she went against the social norms of the time and insisted that all four were given the same opportunities to study and pursue their dreams. In fact, she raised her four daughters to be independent and to think for themselves, often going against the objections of her strict husband. Mercedes encouraged her daughters to pursue their passions and to speak up for themselves, something that can be extremely dangerous in a state ruled by political censorship.

Patria Mercedes

The oldest sister, Patria Mercedes, was born on February 27, 1924. Her birth date coincided with the anniversary of the nation's independence, so she was named Patria, which means 'fatherland'. As she grew older, she expressed the desire to become a nun and at the age of 14 was sent to a Catholic boarding school, the Colegio Inmaculada Concepción, in La Vega. After three years, she gave up her desire to serve the church and married the farmer Pedro Gonzales. The couple would go on to have four children: Nelson Enrique, Noris Mercedes, Raul Ernesto, and Juan Antonio (who died five months after his birth).

Patria continued to indulge in her passion for art and painting while raising her children and her husband would later support her in the fight against the Trujillo regime. For their involvement in trying to overthrow the dictator, the family had their property and home seized by the authorities. Nonetheless, Patria continued her anti-government efforts, although she was never imprisoned.

Clearly committed to the cause, she has been quoted as saying; *"We cannot allow our children to grow up in this corrupt and tyrannical regime. We have to fight against it, and I am willing to give up everything, even my life if necessary."* From her words, we can assume that although she was extremely aware of the risks she was taking, she continued to struggle against tyranny regardless of the consequences to herself or her family.

She was murdered, along with her other two sisters, in 1960.

Minerva Argentina

Minerva Argentina was the second Mirabal sister, born on March 12, 1926. It's Minerva who initially became involved with the underground movement to overthrow the government, after having her eyes opened to the atrocities being carried out by the regime while away at school. She was allowed to go with Patria to the Colegio Inmaculada Concepción and it's there that she first met girls whose families had been tortured at the hands of Trujillo's men. The sense of injustice must have been quite a shock to her after growing up in a rather insular rural environment and certainly incited her enough to want to take action.

She was known for her rebellious nature and hatred of wrongdoing, so it was only a matter of time before she was immersing herself in the underground movement against the regime. Her political awakening found a platform when she went to the University in Santo Domingo after being granted the right to study Law. She was the first woman to be accepted to study this male-dominated profession but was denied the right to practice on graduating and never received her diploma.

It was during her university years that she met her future husband, Manuel Tavarez Justo, who was also an anti-Trujillo activist. Together, they became involved with the Popular Socialist Party and began fighting for freedom. The couple married on November 20, 1955, and moved to Monte Cristi, where they had two children; Minu and Manolito. Her family obligations as mother and wife didn't prevent Minerva from continuing the political struggle and she was subsequently arrested and harassed multiple times on the orders of Trujillo himself.

Despite that, she was adamant that she would do whatever she could to release her fellow countrymen and women from tyrannical rule and was prepared to do whatever it took to achieve that goal. At one point, while under detention, she was told she would be set free if she slept with Trujillo. Of course, she refused and was later placed under house arrest for three years, as well as suffering repeated harassment from El Jefe.

She was savagely beaten and strangled, along with her two sisters, in 1960.

Antonia Maria Teresa

Antonia Maria Teresa (Maté) was the youngest sister, born on October 15, 1936. She also went to the Colegio Inmaculada Concepción and graduated from the Liceo de San Francisco de Macorís in 1954. She later went on to study mathematics at the University of Santo Domingo and married the engineer Leandro Guzman on February 14, 1958. They had one daughter together and, just like her sisters, she became involved in activities against the corrupt Trujillo government.

Maté also suffered for her radicalism, being arrested and detained at the infamous La Cuarenta prison alongside Minerva in 1960 for her involvement in a conspiracy that would later become known as the June 14 Revolutionary Movement. After being transferred to La Victoria prison, the two sisters were freed, only to be locked up a few days later in La Cuarenta again. They were sentenced to five years for threatening the security of the state but were eventually freed on August 18, 1960. Her

29

words reveal her bravery: *"... perhaps what we have most near is death, but that idea does not frighten me, we shall continue to fight for that which is just... "*

Maté was only 25 years old when she was violently murdered on November 1960, along with Minerva and Patria.

Bélgica Adela

Bélgica Adela (Dedé) was the second child of the Mirabal family but, unlike her sisters, she never attended college or university. Instead, she took a more traditional role, marrying Jaime Fernandez and raising three children while helping out in the family business. It is said that the main reason she wasn't involved in any political activity against Trujillo is that her husband didn't allow her to do so. Nonetheless, her decision to bring up the children of her sisters after their murder in 1960 is truly inspiring.

Not only that; she was the 'unknown Mariposa' who continued to carry the torch for her sisters' sacrifices for more than 50 years before her own death in 2014. Dedé worked tirelessly to keep her sisters' stories alive and to speak out about injustice all over the world. She established the Mirabal Sisters Foundation in 1992 and opened the Mirabal Sisters Museum in the family home in 1994. The museum still receives thousands of visitors each year and Dedé continued to lead tours there until she passed away at the age of 88 in 2014.

A family loss

There's no doubt that the whole family was severely affected by the death of their father, Enrique, on his release from prison in 1953. The stress of the intimidation and worry about the safety of his daughters must have been too much for him, and his passing would have only made his daughters even more determined to see justice in their homeland. He suffered because his daughter rejected the insatiable lust of Trujillo but his death gave the Mirabal sisters even more incentive to fight for freedom.

Having said that, they tried to maintain stable family lives as much as possible, raising their children and hoping for a better future. When you look at photographs of these young women, you are struck by their obvious beauty, each one worthy of Hollywood status. One fascinating photograph dated around 1949 features Minerva sitting in a Jeep, with Patria and Maté at her side. Each woman has a style of their own, sporting chic sunglasses, stylish slacks, frilly dresses, and the fashionable hairstyles of the day. The images evoke a sense of warm nostalgia and are snapshots into a carefree past of three beautiful young women in the prime of their lives.

Their roles as mothers and wives didn't prevent them from actively seeking to bring down the oppressive El Jefe. Their story is not unlike those of thousands of women all over the world who have struggled against dictatorships and tyranny through various means. From being armed guerilla fighters to organizing clandestine activities aimed at bringing about democracy, women have always played their part in the political arena. How they do it depends on the circumstances but being mothers, daughters, sisters, and wives, has never been an obstacle.

The Mirabal sisters were intelligent, well-educated, free-thinking, and passionate. It was evident to them that the sociopolitical situation in their country was unacceptable and they had first-hand experience of the barbarity of the regime. It is, therefore, no surprise that they were prepared to fight to overcome that. Minerva, in particular, must have often felt she was the target of Trujillo's backlash after rebuffing his advances at the party they were all invited to. No matter what coercion was applied, she refused to give in to the sexual advances of the dictator and continued to be a thorn in his side.

The refusal

There are several different accounts of what really happened at that party, but the general belief is that when Trujillo spotted Minerva and made a move on her, she reacted badly. A loud exchange ensued and while some say that she actually slapped him in the face, others claim she rejected him without any such act of violence. Whichever version is correct, it would result in Trujillo starting a vicious campaign against the family as a whole. Despite Minerva's father sending letters of apology to Trujillo about his daughter's behavior, he was imprisoned and underwent terrible torture. The deprivation he suffered while in jail meant that he was never the same man after his release and his health eventually deteriorated until he died in 1953.

When Minerva and her mother were put under house arrest in a hotel, she agreed to meet with Trujillo, who attempted to force her to have sex with him to secure their release. She refused him once more and managed to escape, which must have brought on great wrath and a thirst for vengeance on his part. Not only was he rebuked once by this insolent woman but several times. Perhaps Minerva had sealed her fate at that moment, for Trujillo's retaliation against the Mirabal family was endless. Their business suffered as a result, with people too afraid to have dealings with a family that had upset the president for fear of reprisals. And despite Minerva graduating at the top of her class in university, she was prohibited from practicing law by Trujillo, who personally saw to it that she wasn't granted a license.

It does make you wonder who really had the power here. Obviously, Trujillo controlled every aspect of political, social, and economic life in the Dominican Republic throughout the years of terror. But it must have infuriated him to know that he couldn't have everything he wanted, including Minerva Mirabal. His impotence as the 'Big Man' must have played havoc on his deranged ego and caused him to come down even harder on all those who resisted him.

Mirabal detested Trujillo and was the first sister to strongly voice her anti-Trujillo opinions. Patria and Maté were soon to follow while Dede remained largely removed from the activism. Nevertheless, she too played a part in her own way after the murders by bringing up her late sisters' children and retelling their story for the world to hear.

Holding the torch

Talking about her sisters many years later, Dedé is quoted as saying: *"They each had their own reasons for revolution, whether to fight for a better country, for justice, freedom, or simply just a better life for their children. They were living in forced poverty, fear, oppression… It was like continuously pushing them down. They all had an inner fire, a desire to get back up after getting pushed down. They managed to look deep inside themselves and find what they really and truly wanted."*

It is through Dedé that we can recall what really happened to the Mariposas and her contribution to preserving their legacy should not be forgotten.

The sisters must have been living in a constant state of fear about what would happen to their families and loved ones if their activities against the regime were exposed. Despite that, nothing could dissuade them from their commitment to overthrowing oppression in their country and they would have been highly driven by the atrocities that they themselves witnessed.

There could have been no doubt in the minds of those three young women that they were going to be killed when their car was ambushed on the way back from visiting husbands in prison on November 25, 1960. Knowing how ruthless Trujillo's henchmen were, it must have been a moment of sheer terror to face death on that fateful day and we can only imagine what suffering they went through.

Their resistance had invoked the wrath of the tyrant but the act was to eventually bring him to his knees.

CHAPTER 4
THE BUTTERFLIES

"Just living is not enough," said the butterfly.
"One must have sunshine, freedom and a little flower."
—*Hans Christian Anderson*

Women played an essential part in the resistance movement against Trujillo during his three decades of rule. As the anti-government movement became more organized and vocal, many women's voices could be heard. They challenged the dictators' rhetoric of putting family first when, in reality, he was destroying the Dominican home with his violent oppression.

The Mirabal sisters were not alone in their struggle, and they had the support of many other women who were engaged in political activities to end the rape of the country. As Professor Myrna Herrera Mora points out in her work, *Dominican Women: 1930-1961*, many women were engaged in the struggle from neighboring countries like Puerto Rico. A demonstration even took place in Cuba in 1959 in support of the Dominican women and mothers and calling for an end to the 'Jackal's' rule.

In fact, women were operating at both local, national, and international levels, putting themselves and their families in great danger. Although Trujillo's eventual downfall may have been orchestrated partly through international intervention, we shouldn't ignore the valiant women who had brought attention to barbarity throughout the years. His failure to maintain the link between traditional family values and family unity was highlighted, exposing how he had destroyed thousands of families. Those women who were vocal brought this raw reality into the public debate.

Bearing witness

As Trujillo established an even tighter grip on all freedom of expression towards the last decade of his rule, many Dominicans were forced into exile and continued to raise their voices from afar. Women wanted to bear witness to the atrocities taking place in their country and were aware of the need to bring international attention to the regime's abuse of power.

We can assume that the Mirabal sisters felt part of that movement, but had to be extremely cautious in how they participated in the resistance. It's one thing to be living in exile, and quite another to be living under the very nose of the tyrant, with his spies lurking around every corner. The women who bravely opposed Trujillo were also challenging the Spanish-Colonial ideals of womanhood and what it meant in their Dominican society.

Their story continues to resonate with modern audiences today and accounts of their story in books such as *The Time of The Butterflies* and the 2001 movie of the same name brought their achievements to a wider audience. More than 60 years after their deaths, they remain as vanguards of feminine opposition to masculine power. Living in a society of strict gender roles and expectations, the Mirabals and many other women challenged what they saw as extreme oppression and 'patriarchal' authority.

The time for change

Trujillo's relationship with women mirrored the historical treatment of women in the Dominican Republic, which was entrenched in a Spanish Colonial lens of going back centuries. Women had traditionally been seen as weaker, less rational, and more emotional than men, and their roles were tied to those of marriage and motherhood. Without much access to education, their usefulness was restricted to housekeeping, fidelity, and the rearing of their children.

These colonial ideas continued to pervade Dominican society well into the 20th century, with a push against the modernization of women influenced by American values. The idea that women were equal to men was seen as unacceptable for the most part and those influenced by American culture were seen as too bold for their own good. Trujillo advocated this traditional notion of women's place in the society and reinforced the idea of women being the center of the traditional family and national morality.

The Mirabal sisters, like many middle-class women of their era, were opposed to this kind of old-fashioned thinking and rejected it outright. They wanted their independence and embraced the opportunity to receive an education and bring about political change. The three sisters proved that they were capable, rational, and politically astute, which went against everything Trujillo demanded women should be. He expected subservience, docility, and domesticity.

In her memoir *Vivas en su jardín*, Dedé Mirabal recounted that Patria used her house as a meeting place for the clandestine operations, with people from all over the country coming to sit around the table. This kind of activism flew in the face of Trujillo's refusal to allow women any power within the political sphere. Even when their husbands were imprisoned after the failed assassination attempt of Trujillo in January 1960, their political activity didn't stop and Minerva earned herself a reputation for being one of the most active revolutionaries by the Trujillo regime.

No doubt the 'Big Man' recalled with some disdain the fact that this woman had also already defied him several times in the past by rebuking his sexual advances. That must have hurt his ego a lot.

A woman's place

Trujillo was a shrewd man though and understood from the very beginning of his rule that he needed elite women on his side. He even went as far as recognizing the newly formed feminist group Acción Feminista Dominicana and granted women full suffrage in 1942 in an attempt to secure their loyalty to him. As 'Father of the New Nation', he was determined to create an image of empowering women so that they could carry out their traditional maternal roles within the family. Despite women gaining a foot in the door of the establishment, the reality was that they were up against a totalitarian state that had no regard whatsoever for civil liberties.

A lot of the female opponents of Trujillo rejected the conservative maternal stereotypes that he was trying to promote and saw any support for him as untenable. The underground resistance offered them an opportunity to vent their dislike of his policies and a platform through which to bring attention to his hypocrisy. This is how Minerva first began her journey into political life and was no doubt incensed by the double standards of the time. She was an educated, ambitious woman who had seen how the dictator trampled over anyone who didn't fall in with his desires.

She would have been aware of the many women shrouded in black, mourning the loss of family members at the hands of the regime, and witnessed the anguish of those who were left without breadwinners and loved ones. Minerva would also come to learn about the resistance movement which had begun in the 1940s that had been subsequently silenced, with many activists fleeing the country for fear of retribution.

Education and revolt

The 1950s saw a resurgence of opposition on home soil in the University of San Domingo where she was studying. More and more women were now able to enter higher education, with many of them becoming more radicalized at the same time. Minerva would have been one of many female students who were involved in political activism and on her first arrest in 1949, the event drew a lot of media attention from outside the Dominican Republic. In an era when the rest of the world was looking forward to liberty earned after the second world war, it seemed inconceivable that young women were being arrested for speaking out against a known dictator.

At first, women weren't treated as harshly as men when imprisoned and the extent to which they were politically active was grossly underestimated for a long time. The regime became conscious of how it would come across to its international backers if it was too heavy-handed with female inmates. Towards the end of the dictatorship, multiple reports of female prisoners being manhandled, assaulted, humiliated, and denied suitable conditions of internment came to light. The news sparked outrage amongst public opinion, which saw through the charade of Trujillo promoting the nation as a family while flaunting those standards by ill-treating women.

On her release, Minerva continued her clandestine activities and was even allowed to return to law school on the condition that she gave a speech exalting Trujillo as a great leader. The promise of completing her degree was obviously more important to her than having to pander to his ego for once and she went on to complete her studies with high marks. It must have felt like a harsh blow not to be awarded her certificate and Trujillo's obvious pettiness in not allowing her to work must have infuriated her. It's also possible that she understood she was being scapegoated by the goat himself, who wanted to set an example to other women that they shouldn't resist him, or else...

Going underground

When Minerva married Manuel Tavarez Justo in 1955, she and her other two sisters became even more involved in the underground resistance. The couple sought support in Manuel's hometown of Monte Cristi until pressure from the regime and her second pregnancy forced them to return to her family home in Ojo de Agua where she continued to operate. She formed contacts with the catholic organization known as Acción Clero Cultural, a resistance group posing as Trujillo supporters, and was soon meeting in secret with her husband and sisters to set up a nationwide resistance movement.

Events going on in Cuba no doubt fuelled the optimism that Minerva and her companions felt. They would have known about the struggles of the revolutionary Fidel Castro to overthrow the notorious Fulgencio Batista. Minerva is even quoted as saying that there was just as much sentiment against Trujillo as there was against Batista in Cuba, and she was optimistic that they could achieve the same success if organized.

In June of 1959, events occurred that were to spark a shift in the status quo. A small group of exiled insurgents backed by Castro arrived from Cuba and attacked the towns of Constanza, Maimon, and Estero Hondo. The government was tipped off about their movements and the military confronted them, killing most of the insurgents. This failed invasion inspired the 14th of June Movement, which Minerva and her sisters joined and it was Minerva herself who drew up the original declaration of principles for the movement. Although admired for her leadership skills, she wasn't given that official title but was certainly a driving force behind the new movement.

Incarceration and torture

Referred to within the underground movement by the code name Las Mariposas (The Butterflies), the sisters soon became known to the secret police for their plan to overthrow Trujillo and were arrested but released after a short time. Hundreds of supporters of the June 14th Movement were rounded up and brutally tortured and women weren't exempt this time. Eye witness testimonies spoke of women prisoners being forced to parade naked in front of male detainees, tortured with metal prods, and indecently assaulted.

They were fed slops and given little water, woken up in the middle of the night to be interrogated, placed in solitary confinement, moved from one prison to another, not allowed visitors, and often packed into tiny cells without air or proper ventilation. They were forced to witness the torture of their husbands, brothers, or fellow compatriots, and sentenced to as long as 30 years in prison during dubious trials. It's no wonder that the Mirabal sisters were even more determined to continue their fight against the tyrannical ruler after suffering so much pain and torture.

Indeed, the treatment of female political prisoners shocked the whole nation as stories began to leak out of what they were being subjected to. The inhumanity of the regime was in stark contradiction to its slogans of family values and decency, creating much outrage from both domestic commentators and international observers.

The brutality of the government caused a dramatic increase in the numbers of people wanting to join the resistance and information was spread silently throughout the country, with people being recruited from all different socioeconomic backgrounds and professions. The bulk of the student activists were middle-class and not all were supported by their families. It was an era of fear and mistrust, often with family members or servants being part of the military regime or spies. Within that context, it was crucial that information relating to any activity was kept to a minimum number of people.

Supporters of the movement would hand out leaflets and pamphlets in the streets, hold clandestine meetings in churches, and sometimes make public declarations, which was very risky. The aim of the movement was to bring democracy to the country and have a freely elected government, as well as the implementation of economic revisions. News of the opponents being imprisoned and tortured was disseminated by those released and their testimonies would eventually lead former international allies to withdraw support for Trujillo.

It seems as if he began to lose control of his sanity in the last 18 months of his rule, with mass arrests forcing even the Church (up until now a staunch ally) to speak out against him. When six bishops proposed an amnesty for political prisoners, the police were ordered to round up hundreds of people said to be involved in a conspiracy against the state, and Trujillo even entertained the idea of killing the Pope himself.

The Church sent out a letter that was to be read at every Mass in the country on January 31, 1960, condemning the blatant violation of human rights. The resistance movement took on more support as waves of indignation rippled throughout the nation and the time was approaching for the dictator to fall. Around that time, Trujillo is said to have stated that his only two problems were the Church and the Mirabal sisters, and no doubt he thought that by getting rid of the latter, he would solve half of it.

Terror tactics

El Jefe was no stranger to brutal oppression and employed gangs of murderers known as La 42 to do his dirty work for him. They would drive through the streets in red cars, putting fear into the soul of every innocent citizen, and he kept a death list of those he wanted to be taken out. His paranoia knew no bounds and the secret police (SIM, the Servicio de Inteligencia Militar), orchestrated the murder of the Mirabal sisters. He even approved an assassination attempt on the Venezuelan President Rómulo Ernesto Betancourt Bello, leading to the blocking of his sugar quota profits by the United States.

Desperate men will do desperate things and the murder of the Mirabal sisters on November 25 in 1960 sparked a wave of protests when the truth was uncovered. The emperor was now wearing no clothes and had nowhere to hide his brutality.

Chapter 5
The 'Accident'

"If they kill me… I'll reach my arms out through my tomb
and I'll be even stronger."
–Minerva Mirabal

On November 25th 1960, Patria, Minerva and Maria Teresa were happily returning home. They had been visiting the prison of Fortaleza San Felipe in Puerto Plata, where the husbands of Patria and Minerva were being held. Maria Teresa had gone along with them for moral support, even though her husband was still incarcerated in the capital. The women would have been in high spirits as they drove along the mountain road to Salcedo with their driver, Rufino de la Cruz.

Rufino wasn't just any old driver; he had affiliations with the 14th of June movement and was someone that the family trusted. His belief in their cause meant he felt a responsibility to accompany them on their trip to the prison when asked to do so. Everyone knew that the Mariposas were marked targets of Trujillo and yet, Rufino was willing to escort them that day, as he had done several times in the past. When he agreed to drive the girls to see their husbands, it wasn't just as a driver but also as a protector. His heroism had often been overlooked but now his bravery is truly acknowledged and he is known by his name rather than just as 'the driver' of this vicious attack.

Living in fear

Even though they tried to live as normal a life as possible, the Mirabals would have always been conscious of the fact that they could be arrested again. The risk was ever-present but the thought that they would all be slaughtered? This must have seemed too far-fetched, even to them. Who, in their right mind, would execute such a savage act? So far, Trujillo had not gone about murdering women in cold blood, although he often had adversaries murdered and their deaths staged as traffic accidents, which was a tried and tested formula.

There isn't enough information available from the time to clarify if Minerva was the primary target or if they all were, although we do know that the husbands of Minerva and Maria Teresa, Manolo and Leandro, had just been transferred to Puerto Plata prison from Santo Domingo. On their way to and from the prison, the sisters would have to pass a notoriously dangerous highway known for its frequent accidents so it seems like a well-hatched plan by the Trujillo regime.

Some observers who knew the sisters at the time claim that they had known about the threat of being ambushed, but had decided to make the trip anyway. Family members had also warned them to be cautious, although Minerva was convinced that the fact they were women would prevent them from falling into any grave danger.

As they waved goodbye to their children, leaving them in the care of Aunt Dedé, the three Mirabals couldn't possibly have imagined that they would never hold their loved ones again. Despite being committed to the cause, they wouldn't have been willingly reckless and must have weighed up the risks very carefully before departing for the prison visit. Even though they had heard the rumors of a possible murder attempt, it's possible that they couldn't envisage such a blatant act of violence and and decided to make the trip with the help of Rufino del la Cruz.

The ambush

Most of the accounts of what happened on that fateful night come from the witness testimonials of those later accused of the murders. Víctor Alicinio Peña Rivera, Trujillo's right-hand man, along with Ciriaco de la Rosa, Ramon Emilio Rojas, Alfonso Cruz Valeria, and Emilio Estrada Malleta, were all members of the secret police. The order must have come from Trujillo himself, for it could not have been carried out without his say so, being the highest authority in the land. As the witness Ciriaco de la Rosa pointed out during his trial, *"I tried to prevent the disaster, but I could not because if I had he, Trujillo, would have killed us all."*

De la Rosa also gave a chilling account of what happened that night, saying that after the girl's jeep was intercepted, he ordered his henchmen to pick up sticks and take out the girls. His co-assassin, Alfonso Cruz, pulled out Minerva and Maletta grabbed Rufino. The men forced the Mirabal Sisters into their car when another vehicle with employees of the Dominican Social Security Fund approached them. Patria managed to break free for a moment and told the social security workers who they were, asking them to notify their family about what was happening.

She was grabbed by her assassin, who ordered the workers not to talk about what they had witnessed and they were allowed to drive away. The four victims were then driven to a sugar cane grove on the end of the road, leaving Perez Terrero as a lookout in case anyone else drove by.

All four of the victims were separated and strangled to death before being savagely beaten on the mountain road between Puerto Plata and Santiago.

After the three sisters and their driver were so callously murdered, their bodies were thrown back into the jeep. It was then pushed over the cliff at a remote spot near La Cumbre into the gorge below to make it look like an unfortunate accident.

Patria was 36 years old, Minerva was 34 years old, Maria was 25 years old, and Rufino de la Cruz was 37 years old.

The cover up

When the sisters failed to return that evening, the family quickly came to the conclusion that something must have happened to them and their worst fears became a reality. Dedé received news of her sisters' deaths early the next morning. She went to the local police station with her husband and received a telegram saying: '*Patria Mirabal, Maria Teresa Mirabal, Rufino de la Cruz, and one other person have died in a fatal traffic accident*'.

Minerva's name wasn't mentioned, highlighting once again Trujillo's resentment against the woman who had said 'no' to him too many times. It was almost as if he was trying to wipe out any memory of her, while causing further unbearable pain to her family. Such was his manipulative grip that, days later, their mother Doña Chea was forced to sign a letter that was published in the local newspaper confirming the death of her daughters was accidental.

It wasn't that clear what had happened at first, although most people believed that Trujillo was behind the murder. Although the kidnapping and murder constituted the most outrageous crime committed during his lengthy dictatorship, the evil act would not immediately come to light. Nevertheless, when it became apparent what had really happened, the sisters' deaths would have exactly the opposite effect of what Trujillo wanted.

The fact that Trujillo wanted these women killed is a telling sign of their significance. On the one hand, it proves how threatened he felt by their activities within the resistance movement and what lengths he was willing to go to in order to silence the opposition. On the other hand, it reveals just how influential they, like many other women, were in the struggle against the regime. He certainly would not have been able to stand knowing just how much they vilified him. Perhaps he wished to make an example of them and send out a warning to anyone opposing him that they too would meet with his deadly wrath. But instead of silencing the opposition, he eventually brought about his own downfall.

Treasuring their memory

If you find yourself on the road to La Cumbre today, you will come across the 'Mirabal sisters pilgrimage trail', which marks the exact location where the sisters were brutally murdered.

There isn't much to see at the end of the dirt track apart from a monument made of three tall concrete spikes and three bronze busts of the sisters. Each bust has a plaque bearing the name and date of birth of the women and information about their deaths. The busts don't do justice to how beautiful they were in real life but at least they serve as a place of pilgrimage where their memory is still preserved.

A large balcony overlooks the verdant valley below where the sister's car was pushed down. The summit, (in Spanish, la cumbre) is a poignant spot where each visitor has the opportunity to pause and reflect on the brutality of the horrific episode.

The three sisters certainly took on great status years after their deaths, becoming national symbols of heroism and bravery. Much of this was due to the concerted efforts of the surviving sister, Dedé, who once said that she had been spared from death in order to live to tell their tale. She also took on the role of bringing up her sisters' children and dedicated her life to keeping their memory alive in the public eye.

The Mirabal sisters are now buried in their family home in Ojo de Agua, which Dedé turned into a museum known as Casa Museo Hermanas Mirabal. The house is surrounded by a large, beautifully curated garden where visitors can admire the orchids and artificial butterflies scattered throughout. Items on display inside the home include the long braid of Marie Teresa and a bloodstained handkerchief recovered after the murder, as well as family photos, clothes, and everyday objects. Visitors can get a true sense of the sister's daily lives on visiting the museum and it adds to the realization that these were very normal women who had extraordinary lives.

Every November 25th, the Hermanas Mirabal Foundation organizes various events in the museum garden to honor Patria, Minerva and María Teresa, with speeches and floral tributes. On the same day, the 'March of the Butterflies' takes place, bringing together thousands of people demanding the cessation of violence against women.

In 2007, Salcedo province, one of the 32 provinces in the Dominican Republic and home to the sisters, changed its name to Hermanas Mirabal province. The Hermanas Mirabal station of the Santo Domingo Metro is named in their honor and the 200 Dominican pesos bill features their images, while a stamp has also been issued in their memory.

A 137-foot obelisk built by Trujillo in 1935 to commemorate the renaming of the capital city from Santo Domingo to Ciudad Trujillo is now covered with murals by local artists dedicated to the sisters and they are considered to be national heroines by all on the island to this day.

The sisters even have a street named after them in one of New York's largely Dominican neighborhood. The southeast corner of 168th St. and Amsterdam Avenue in Washington Heights was officially co-named Mirabal Sisters Way by the Council of the city of New York in 2019. There is also a school campus in Washington Heights, Manhattan called the Mirabal Sisters Campus.

Globally recognized as symbols of social justice and feminism, the sisters have inspired the creation of many organizations that focus on keeping their legacy alive through social actions. One of these organizations is the Mirabal Sisters Cultural and Community Center; a non-profit organization that seeks to improve the status of immigrant families.

It's truly amazing to think that these three women made such a lasting impact, not only on the political situation in their own country, but that they also merged as feminist icons in the fight for an end to violence against women throughout the world.

While their murder was crude, shameful, and criminal, their lives inspire honor, strength, and rightousness for women all over the globe.

Retelling the story

Although their murders played a pivotal part in the history of the Dominican Republic of that era, much of what we knew about the Mirabal sisters until recently could only be gleamed through fictional works such as *Los que falsificaron la firma de dios (They Forged the Signature of God*, 1993) by Dominican writer Viriato Sención, *La Fiesta Del Chivo* (The Feast of the Goat, 2000) by Peruvian writer Mario Vargas Llosa, *In the Time of the Butterflies* (1994) by Dominican-American writer Julia Alvarez, and *The Farming of Bones* (1998) by Haitian-American writer Edwidge Danticat.

The above works all give accounts of the repression going on at that time, the state-sponsored atrocities, the Parsley Massacre, and the murder of the Mirabal sisters. They illustrate the collective trauma of the Dominican people and expose the workings of a military dictatorship. Trujillo had complete control of the press, so most official discourse presented a totally obscured picture of what was really going on in the country during his rule. Despite that, the murder of the Mirabals couldn't be covered up.

Such a wicked and violent act against women was not only shocking but also completely unacceptable for the public at large. They had stomached the massacre of the Haitians to a certain extent, swallowing Trujillo's rhetoric that the country was fighting a battle with blacks who wanted to overrun their country. His brainwashing techniques were decidedly pointed and aimed at perpetuating a sense of fear among the public.

The narrative of 'fake news' helped Trujillo to suppress criticism and his well-oiled propaganda machine was very successful. It wasn't until the above books were published that the international audience began to gain a different perspective on what really happened during his dictatorship, putting the Mirabal sisters on center stage.

Trujillo combined all the traits of the proverbial Latin American dictator and we find similar figures in works by the writers Gabriel García Marquez, Alejo Carpentier, Augusto Roa Bastos, and Miguel Angel Asturias. He epitomized everything that we now come to recognize about the nature of dictatorship in general. Although many factors came into play during Trujillo's downfall, the cowardly killing of three beautiful women in such a manner had a greater effect on Dominicans than most of his other crimes and it was something they just could not forgive. It also caught the attention of the international press, putting pressure on the U.S. to step in.

Six months later, Trujillo was assassinated by military leaders in his own army.

CHAPTER 6
THE BEGINNING OF THE END

"In every tyrant's heart there springs in the end this poison,
that he cannot trust a friend."
—Aeschylus

On May 30 1960, a spy working in the garage where Trujillo's 1957 Chevrolet was parked tipped off conspirators that El Jefe was planning to meet his lover, Mona Sanchez, later that evening.

General Juan Tomás Díaz, Pedro Livio Cedeño, Antonio de la Maza, Amado García Guerrero, Roberto Pastoriza, Huáscar Tejeda, General Antonio Imbert Barrera, Salvador Estrella Sadhalá, and the Presidential Guard Lieutenant Amado García Guerrero were engaged in the plot. General José René (Pupo) Román was also later implicated although he wasn't present during the attack.

Four or five of the conspirators equipped themselves out with revolvers, pistols, a sawn-off shotgun, and two semi-automatic rifles, some of which we later learn had been supplied by the CIA. They lay in wait for Trujillo on a quiet part of the road leading to San Cristobal.

At 8pm, Trujillo made a visit to his mother, Julia Molina, before taking a stroll accompanied by several of his henchmen. He then visited his daughter Angelita before getting into his Chevrolet Bel Air to go to San

Cristóbal. The conspirators were following his movements and when they saw the car passing by the Agua y Luz Theater, they knew this was their chance.

Trujillo and his chauffeur got into the Chevrolet at 10 pm and proceeded to drive to Sanchez's house. El Jefe was dressed as he usually did — with military clothing — so he was even easier to spot. When the Chevrolet approached the location where the assassins lay in wait, Antonio de la Maza fired the first shot and then García Guerrero also opened fire. Huáscar Tejera and Pedro Livio Cedeño joined the attack and the exchange of rounds lasted for about ten minutes.

El Jefe ordered his driver to stop to fight back and the chauffeur returned fire with two machine guns he carried in the car with him. Trujillo was badly wounded in the attack but managed to climb out of the car. Seeing that he was still alive, de la Maza and Imbert doubled back and although Trujillo also retaliated with a 38 he was carrying, he couldn't match the fire power of the assailants. He was shot several more times before falling to the ground and by 10.10 pm, it was all over.

Pastoriza helped del la Maza to put El Jefe's body in the trunk of a black Chevrolet and drove back to the city, parking it two blocks away from the American consulate.

After the event, the assassins scattered as a massive manhunt began in search of the attackers. Trujillo's playboy son, Ramfis, flew back from Paris to take over and he ordered the secret police to round up, detain and torture hundreds of possible suspects. Trujillo's son and the regime were skilled in handling disinformation and made sure to manipulate the narrative of the event, accusing the plotters of being ambitious traitors and disloyal to the dictator Trujillo. Their smear campaign was initially believed by some and it convinced them to accept that the assassination was not inspired by any notions of patriotism.

Those deemed responsible for the assassination were summarily executed in the Hacienda Maria Massacre. Some accounts also state that other conspirators were thrown into the sea to be eaten by sharks. Imbert managed to escape the death penalty by securing asylum in the Italian Embassy and another co-conspirator named Luis Amiama Tió is also thought to have survived.

Despite the efforts of the Trujillo family to maintain control of the country after the death of El Jefe, they ultimately failed. A military uprising in November of the same year and the threat of American intervention finally brought an end to the 30 year regime. President Joaquín Antonio Balaguer Ricardo, the puppet of Trujillo who had been appointed in 1957, allowed Trujillo's son to relocate his father's body to Paris, and then later to a cemetery near Madrid. Balaguer continued to rule in true caudillo style after Trujillo's death, carrying out acts of state terrorism, rigging elections, and the torturing and killing of thousands of political opponents.

The 'ajusticiamiento'
From what we know today, the assassination of Trujillo was actually organized by more than 50 people. The act is often referred to as the 'execution', or 'ajusticiamiento', which can also be translated as cessation, or bringing to an end of something. There were also many conspirators indirectly linked to the plot and it was no means a random act carried out by terrorists. Nor was it planned by the underground resistance movement, but by those closest to Trujillo himself. These men were later heralded as national heroes by the Dominican people and their bravery is still honored today.

García Guerrero and Imbert Barrera were wounded during the altercation and Cedeño needed medical assistance. He was the first of the conspirators to be arrested. General Román was also detained and suffered atrocious torture before being shot by the dictator's son. Although the second part of the plan, which was to carry out a coup d'état, was not to be, an era of repression marked by imprisonment, intimidation, and torture had come to an end.

The plot of May 30 wasn't the first one that had been hatched to take out Trujillo. Numerous attempts had been made in the past but had failed miserably. On this occasion though, the plan was better organized, carried out with almost military precision, by those who were sick and tired of Trujillos reign of terror and blatant greed - his time had come.

Amongst those directly involved in the conspiracy were Eduardo Antonio García Vásquez, Miguel Ángel Bissié Romero, Ernesto de la Maza Vásquez, Mario de la Maza Vásquez, Bolívar de la Maza Vásquez, Pablo de la Maza Vásquez, Modesto Díaz Quezada, Miguel Ángel Báez Díaz, Manuel from Ovín Filpo, Juan Bautista (Gianni) Vicini Cabral, Ángel Severo Cabral, Donald Read Cabral, Andrés Freites Barreras, Luis Manuel Baquero and Jordi Bossa.

Although it was men at the forefront of the execution, many women also had direct involvement in the plot, including Cristina Díaz, Urania Mueses de Estrella, Guarina Tessón de Imbert, Aída Michel de De la Maza, Hilda Tactuck de De la Maza, Olga Despradel de Cedeño, Marianela Díaz de García, Anneris Malagón, Coffeta Ricart de González, Petra Solano de Rodríguez Echavarría, Flérida Yabra de Berry, Professor Mineta Roque Martínez, Mercedes Amiama Tió, Gracita Díaz de Henríquez, Josefina Padilla de Sánchez, Doctor Gladys de los Santos, Antonia Vásquez de Freites and Josefina Gautier de Álvarez, amongst many others.

By the time of his death, Trujillo's economic empire was unprecedented and his worth was estimated at a vulgar $800 million. He had seized 80% of the Dominican Republic's wealth during his 30-year reign at the expense of the nation's people. The companies he owned employed 45% of the active labor force, meaning that a large percentage of the population depended on him for their livelihood.

Despite the claims of some who came to his defense that he had vastly improved the country's infrastructure and social services, the truth is that he had done so at great cost to the people he was supposed to be serving. His corrupt and nepotistic policies meant that he ranked amongst one of the world's two or three richest individuals in the world in the 1950s, owning 12 palaces and ranches. He shared the spoils amongst his family and they monopolized the whole economy, including the salt, tobacco and beer industries, as well as being the largest landowners.

His children were accredited with ridiculous titles and positions, such as when he crowned his daughter María de los Ángeles de Corazón de Jesús as Queen Angelita I in 1955, and made his son Colonel of the Dominican Army at the age of four.

A period of political turmoil followed Trujillo's death, with more intervention from the United States becoming apparent. The instability led to the election of Juan Emilio Bosch Gaviño in 1963, who was ousted a few months after his inauguration by the military, which was opposed to his socialist ideas. Another junta was put in place until unrest took to the streets of Santo Domingo and the bloody Caamaño Revolt took place in 1965 led by Francisco Alberto Caamaño Deñó. The aim was to restore Juan Bosch as President and establish a constitutional democracy.

On April 28 1965, U.S. Marines and troops from the Organization of American States (OAS) were sent to the Dominican Republic to restore peace and stability and they stayed there until September 1966. Hector Garcia-Godoy was eventually elected as the Provisional President, who is now remembered for his part in returning democracy to the island through organizing the elections of 1966.

The brutal murder of the Mirabal sisters sparked something in the public psyche that it had not witnessed before — intense outrage. Torturing and killing men was one thing, but attacking three young women and savagely beating them to death while trying to stage it as an accident really was too much. It was an attack on every mother, daughter, and sister, done in such a barbaric way that it could not be ignored.

At the same time, many strongmen within the military had become sick and tired of Trujillo's sadistic power plays and wanted him out. In that sense, the Mirabal murders provided the push they needed to bring an end to his reign of terror. He was becoming more of a loose cannon than ever before and no one was safe from his paranoia. The tide of international opposition to Trujillo was also more obvious, and that certainly fuelled the belief that countries like the U.S. would welcome, or even aid any insurgency against him.

Plots and subplots

Trujillo had already fallen out of favor in Washington, when he organized a failed assassination attempt against the Venezuelan President Rómulo Betancourt in 1960. Betancourt had publicly condemned Trujillo's regime and El Jefe, who wasn't going to stand for that, had his secret agents plant a car bomb that killed several people. President Dwight D. Eisenhower was of the belief that Trujillo was just as bad as America's other arch-enemy, Fidel Castro. He ordered the CIA to covertly help the anti-Trujillo elements in the Dominican Republic to overthrow this troublesome dictator. At the same time, economic sanctions were imposed and diplomatic ties with the country were severed, leaving Trujillo feeling ostracized and insecure.

We now know through official sources that the U.S. ambassador Joseph Farland initially made contact with dissident elements in the country, who were asking for firearms. His successor, Henry Dearborn, later told the rebels they would help them to take out Trujillo but could not be seen to be implicated. The CIA sent 12 sterile sniper rifles with telescopic sights to the Dominican Republic, along with 500 rounds of ammunition. Despite that, Dearborn was of the opinion that the dissidents weren't organized enough to carry out any kind of revolutionary activity, although an assassination of Trujillo was a feasible option. A limited invasion plan was also a possibility, although it would require a lot of on-the-ground expertise, making it rather risky.

When John F. Kennedy took over the presidency in 1961, weapons such as machine guns and pistols were sent to the Dominican dissidents, one of which fell into the hands of Antonio de la Maza. After the Bay of Pigs disaster, the Kennedy administration advised the dissidents not to go ahead with the assassination as the political climate was too unstable. Two days before Trujillo's murder, Kennedy had sent a cable to Dearborn telling him the United States did not condone political assassination in any form and that it must not be associated with any attempt on Trujillo's life.

It was too late. The dissidents had waited long enough and were determined to go ahead with their plan. After the assassination, Dearborn messaged Washington stating that it didn't matter if Trujillo was dead, as long as it's the Dominicans who were held responsible. The event was followed by periods of rioting as the country appeared to be on the verge of collapse. The riots in April of 1965 eventually forced President Lyndon

Johnson to dispatch 22,000 American troops to restore order to the island, although the American invasion was heavily criticized throughout Latin America.

While the Mirabal Museum is an oasis of serenity where one can reflect on the tragedy of their violent deaths, the Memorial Museum of Dominican Resistance in Santo Domingo is a bolder reminder of the oppressive regime. Dedicated to the preservation of the struggles faced by several generations during the Trujillo dictatorship, the museum offers a macabre insight into the dark elements of his oppressive state. Dioramas and models of the torture centers have been constructed, including the restoration and extension of Jail Site 9.

Images of prisoners being tortured make it a sombre audio-visual experience while the collection of exhibits, photos, and documents are extremely detailed. The museum is a place to commemorate the fallen heroes who lost their lives in the struggle for democracy in the Dominican Republic and it is also an educational institution that raises awareness among the younger generations about fundamental human rights and freedom of speech.

Perhaps the two museums represent both sides of the same coin in relation to the Dominican Republic. The shocking murder of the Mirabal sisters was an attack on every home and the society could not bear to see any more barbarity. It struck at the very heart of everything they held dear — family, home, and security. The murder was also the match that lit the powder keg, leading to Trujillo being assassinated by members of his own military who had turned against him.

So much brutality and bloodshed throughout the tumultuous history of this Caribbean island came about at a time when the world could no longer support dictators by any name. After the atrocities of the Holocaust and rebuilding of Europe, the 50s and 60s were a time of great social change for the better. Liberty, freedom, and peace were high on the agenda of civilized societies and the Dominicans were ready to fight for those values.

It took years of oppression to reach breaking point and women played an intrinsic part in bringing the Trujillo dictatorship to an end. Their clandestine activities, organizational skills, ability to network in secret, and decades of raising their voices contributed greatly to the overthrow of 'the goat'.

For many, it is hard to forget Trujillo. But the atrocities carried out in his name need to be remembered so that they may never be repeated.

CHAPTER 7
STATE VIOLENCE AND WOMEN

"We still think of a powerful man as a born leader
and a powerful woman as an anomaly."
—*Margaret Atwood*

Why should we care today about what happened to three unknown women on a tiny Caribbean island over 60 years ago?

The Mirabal murders provide the catalyst for the fall of a brutal dictator and help bring democracy to a long-suffering nation, but the implications of their personal tragedy are also more far-reaching than that. Anyone reading their story will recognize a familiar pattern of behavior, or misbehavior, by a powerful individual or body against women. In short, their story is just as relevant today as it was then.

The Mirabals weren't the first women and, unfortunately, won't be the last to suffer violence at the hands of the state. History has shown us that women are frequently the victims of gender-oriented repression, sexual violence, and torture, or are targets of social injustices.

The Latin American story
Latin America has seen its fair share of dictators in the latter half of the 20th century, often with puppet regimes propped up by the U.S. as the world watches on. Crime, corruption, and terror have been the hallmarks

of many men holding the reins, with Trujillo standing out as being the most ruthless of all.

Marcos Pérez Jiménez became dictator of Venezuela in 1948 with a military junta and terrorized the population on a daily basis with the help of National Security. Meanwhile, Alfredo Stroessner's anti-communist government came to replace that of President Federico Chavez in 1954 in Paraguay. His government proceeded to repress constitutional rights and freedoms in order to seize absolute control.

Gustavo Rojas Pinilla staged a coup in 1953 in Colombia with the support of the military and political leaders. He became notorious for his advocacy of state violence and repression. The army also helped Fulgencio Batista to establish a dictatorship in the Cuban 1952 elections before being overthrown by Fidel Castro. The Cuban Revolution had a lot of support until the authoritarian regime began to exercise more and more suppression of opposition and enforce the loss of liberties.

Carlos Castillo Armas came to rule Guatemala after a CIA-backed operation in 1954, after which the population experienced the brutality of his regime until he was assassinated in 1957 by a personal guard. In 1957, Papa Doc, or François Duvalier, was elected into office in Haiti, after which he proceeded to carry out acts of brutal oppression against the public. His particular brand of state terrorism even included using the traditional Haitian fear of voodoo to keep the public in check.

In Bolivia, a series of coups lead to the American-backed Hugo Banzer overthrowing the leftist government and taking power in 1971. The United States also supported Joao Baptista Figueiredo of Brazil, who seized power in 1964 and went on to use widespread suppression against any voices of opposition.

Augusto Pinochet was responsible for the 1973 coup d'état in Chile against Salvador Allende and became notorious for his brutal policies involving the disappearances and murders of thousands of people in military garrisons. In Panama, Manuel Antonio Noriega seized power under the direction of the CIA in 1983. The country was then plunged into a period of corruption, violence, and economic crisis, with Noriega being closely connected to the Medellín Cartel and the trafficking of drugs and arms.

During the 1976 Argentinian coup d'état, President Isabel Perón was overthrown by several senior army officials and the military junta under Lieutenant General Jorge Rafael Videla proceeded to 'disappear' thousands of activists and young people until 1981. The Mothers of La Plaza de Mayo, many of them by now in wheelchairs, still gather each Thursday in the main square to seek justice for their missing children.

On being a 'great' dictator
As Sonia Farid mentioned in her paper, 'Rewriting the Trujillato: Collective Trauma, Alternative History, and the Nature of Dictatorship, the Trujillato era combined the classic features of any dictatorship. There was the persecution of minorities, brutal elimination of opposition, the abuse of power, the cult of personality, patriarchal discourse, and blatant violations of human and women's rights, all with the complicity of religious institutions. We can still see these kinds of political systems being played out today in many parts of the world, so it is safe to assume that there are plenty more 'Mirabals' out there too. From Angola to Chad and Iran to Syria, there are countless Presidents, Prime Ministers, Kings, and Emirs who also wear the 'dictator' hat.

When a single person or party has absolute power, such as Trujillo, it means that they have complete control and can effectively suppress the population to one degree or another. It's often the case that these figures arise like a phoenix from the ashes, bringing hope in times of economic crises, civil war, or unrest, perhaps even after a natural disaster, such as in the Dominican Republic after the hurricane of 1930.

For a dictatorship to hold onto power, the opposition needs to be silenced, and that's usually done by intimidation, imprisonment, violence, or even assassination - all tried and tested methods for muting those who oppose the powers that be. While dictators pretend to allow for certain levels of freedom, the reality is that there is a loss of political choice and autonomy for the population, with the imposing of state-controlled censorship and other restrictions.

Dictators also like to change the constitution to suit themselves, making sure that they and their lackeys benefit from that. A recent example of this type of action is when Vladimir Putin and his party amended the country's constitution concerning the term limits in 2020 to enable him to remain in power until 2036. Under a dictatorship, we also usually find the unethical persecution of minorities for religious or racial reasons, or because of someone's sexual orientation. These witch hunts are mainly carried out by the use of state-controlled secret police, illegal arrests, and even the use of concentration camps.

Many dictatorships are established through military might, during which the armed forces are used to maintain power. Other power grabs are often made through family connections and ties, such as in the case of a monarchy. As history has shown, foreign support or international pressure can help form new power seats or push dictators to take even more extreme measures to protect their position. They are frequently supported by a party or military and can also rely heavily on their own 'charisma' while single-party dictatorships will dominate the government for long periods of time. It is possible for such regimes to be a hybrid of all of the above, as was the case in Pakistan from 1977 to 1988 and El Salvador from 1948 to 1984.

When dictators hold absolute power, in many instances the population has never known anything else, with North Korea or Cameroon being relevant examples. In such a situation, going against the said dictatorship is unthinkable and those inside its walls have no perception of how their country is viewed by the outside world. In fact, the notion of 'dictatorship' can often be unknown to those living under its rule, as external perspectives are completely inaccessible.

Dictatorships today
According to the World Population Review of 2021, 52 nations were said to be ruled by an authoritarian regime or dictator in 2020.

Three of them were in Latin America and South America, 27 in Asia and the Middle East, and 22 in Africa. Dictatorships come in all shapes and sizes, although each one shares common characteristics. From Aleksandr G. Lukashenko of Belarus, often referred to as Europe's last dictator, to the highly controversial Recep Tayyip Erdoğan of Turkey, there is no shortage of powerful men still ruling their countries with iron rods.

Even in states not identified as dictatorships, one can find examples of political oppression (and often violence) against women. Open up any newspaper today and you come across articles about acts of violence, discrimination, intimidation, and even ethnic cleansing. It is very common for women to be targeted and denied their human rights. The fact that young girls in the newly established Taliban government of Afghanistan were forbidden to go to school after the August 2021 withdrawal of the UN forces is a case in point.

Modern dictatorships are usually a male-dominated profession, with wives being nothing more than accessories to the crimes. Men who usurp power are closely linked to the army, more often than not, which may explain why women have not been known to actively acquire power through military coups. There have been many powerful women leaders who have been criticized for their policies, such as Indira Gandhi in India and Jiang Qing in China, but most have been backstage companions of their spouses, like Imelda Markos in the Philippines and Elena Ceauşescu in Romania.

The many faces of violence

The reality is that state violence against women can take many forms and isn't limited to what we would necessarily view as dictatorial regimes. Rape, public flogging and stoning, forced sterilization and abortion, sexual slavery, war rapes, intimidation, and custodial violence by police or other authorities, all constitute cases in which women fall victim to gender-focused crimes. Women of every social stratum can be victims of political or authorized state violence, regardless of their profession, economic status, or political views. Successful women can be just as vulnerable as those living in refugee camps or prisons and institutional violence often takes the form of discriminatory laws and regulations or reproduction policies and matrilineal laws.

It can take quite a while before there is an awareness of what is really going on inside repressive regimes but although women are often targeted, they always find ways to raise their voices in resistance. Today, with access to worldwide events at our fingertips, we all have the ability to learn about what is going on in the world and to be aware of human rights abuses, with social media becoming a powerful weapon. Back in the days of Trujillo, it was extremely easy for governments to cover up atrocities and to project a completely false version of events. Only the victims and their families knew the real truth.

Unfortunately, this kind of state control continues to exist today in several regimes, such as North Korea. According to the organization Human Rights Watch, North Korea is one of the most repressive countries in the world. Its ruler, Kim Jong Un, has rigidly suppressed freedom of expression, religion, peaceful assembly, and association. Political opposition, independent media, NGOs, and trade unions are prohibited while crimes against humanity carried out by the government include extermination, murder, enslavement, torture, rape, and forced abortions. Those said to oppose the government are detained in secret prison camps where they face torture, forced labor, and starvation.

North Korea certainly isn't the only dictatorship still operating in the world but does appear to exhibit many of the classic features mentioned previously, with a personality cult to boot. Just like Trujillo, Kim Jong Un is portrayed as a godlike figure who dominates daily life. State media spews out positive stories about the great leader and school children are brainwashed into singing his praises. His images appear on billboards, buildings, offices, classrooms, and in the form of large statues (more than 500 across North Korea), while his portrait hangs in nearly every home. Although Kim Jong Un's control of the country may be more sophisticated than that of Trujillo's, the methods are the same.

The right to be a woman
State-authorized violence and repression against women continue to be headline news all over the world and we only need to look at the Americas to see examples of this. Even in the Dominican Republic of today, the criminalization of abortion is just one of the issues Dominican women and human rights activists are still trying to grapple with. Since the country's total ban on abortion in 1884, women's health and lives are being put at risk, even when a pregnancy is life-threatening, unviable, or the result of rape or incest. The archaic law means a prison sentence of up

to 2 years for women and girls who have abortions and up to 20 years for medical professionals who offer them, curtailing a woman's right to make her own sexual and reproductive choices.

Abortion bans such as this also contribute to maternal deaths and affect those women and girls from low-income families and rural areas, who have little access to safer abortion methods such as traveling to another country where abortion is legal.

In Argentina, abortion has only just become legal within 14 weeks of gestation (2020). Until recently, abortions in the country were carried out in clandestine situations at great risk to the patient. The World Health Organization actually cited unsafe abortion as one of the leading causes of maternal mortality in Argentina a few years ago. (WHO: Unsafe Abortion Report 2008)

In Brazil, the Bolsonaro administration has openly undermined the human rights of its populace, including denying inclusive education to children with disabilities, introducing policies to curtail sexual and reproductive services, bringing critics to trial, and routinely blocking the social media accounts of those criticizing the government.

In El Salvador, President Nayib Bukele calls himself 'one of the coolest dictators in the world', but his country also has one of the world's highest homicide rates. State security forces commit extrajudicial executions, sexual assaults, and enforced disappearances on a large scale while gangs exercise territorial control, extort residents, and kill, disappear, rape, or displace those who resist them. Girls and women alleged to have had abortions are currently being imprisoned for homicide.

The overall picture may seem bleak as we read reports of human rights abuses and violence against women across the world. The facts also present a very persuasive argument for why we need to remember women like the Mirabal sisters. It is important to recall such atrocities in order to set a baseline for what is and isn't acceptable, which is why their murders continue to be relevant today.

Despite the importance of their story, it took a long time for the sisters to be officially recognized as national heroines when President Joaquin Balaguer stepped into Trujillo's footsteps after his death. The systemic oppression didn't just disappear overnight and although the word on the street was that the assassination of the tyrant was directly linked to the atrocious murder of the three women, they weren't given any official status until 36 years later. When the Republic began to stabilize, the Mirabal sisters were posthumously granted official recognition, even though everyone was already very familiar with their story.

The United Nations Declaration

Such was the horror of the violent execution of the 'butterflies' that the United Nations declared the anniversary of their deaths as the International Day For The Elimination Of Violence Against Women. The announcement resonated with women all over the world who were fighting against injustice and the Mirabal legacy continues to inspire women from all walks of life up to this day.

Each year, beginning on November 25th, the UN organizes 16 days of activism, ending on International Human Rights Day on December 10th. Since 1993, the UN Secretary-General and UN Women have been actively campaigning to prevent and eliminate violence against women and girls around the world, all instigated by the unlawful killings of the Mirabal sisters. Calls for global action to increase awareness, promote advocacy, and create opportunities for discussion on challenges and solutions make up the main content of this UN initiative.

November 25th is also a day to celebrate the gains that have been made in the area of women's rights over the years and to remind us that many women and girls are still being subjected to rape, domestic abuse, and other forms of violence. The Mirabal crime may have been carried out within a political context but women are also subjected to domestic violence on a daily basis. According to the recent figures produced by the UN, 1 in 3 women and girls experience physical or sexual violence in their lifetime, most frequently by an intimate partner. One hundred and thirty-seven women are killed by a member of their family every day and fewer than 40 percent of the women who experience violence seek help of any sort.

We all know that violence against women is very much part of almost every society, from domestic abuse to war crimes, and the International Day For The Elimination Of Violence Against Women is highly instrumental in reminding us of these occurrences. The aim is to help raise awareness of what needs to be changed in order to empower women rather than making them victims.

A global problem
When we consider the global scale of violence against women, it is estimated that 736 million women—that's almost one in three—have been subjected to intimate partner violence, non-partner sexual violence, or both at least once in their life (30 percent of women aged 15 and older).

In 2018, an estimated one in seven women had experienced physical and/or sexual violence from an intimate partner or husband in the past 12 months (that's 13% of women aged 15 to 49). Globally, 6% of women report they have been subjected to sexual violence from someone other than their husband or partner. However, the true facts about non-partner sexual violence are likely to suggest a much higher figure. Crimes against women include death at the hands of a family member such as a spouse or former intimate partner, with 137 women being killed under these circumstances every day.

Usually, women experiencing violence do not seek help of any kind or will look to family and friends for support, rather than formal institutions such as the police. Global violence tends to occur more in low and lower-middle-income countries and regions, with 37% of women living in countries described as least developed being subject to physical and/or sexual violence at the hands of an intimate partner.

Even though at least 155 countries have passed laws on domestic violence and 140 have laws on sexual harassment in the workplace, this does not guarantee that they are always compliant with international standards and recommendations, or that the laws are implemented and enforced.

From human trafficking for the purpose of sexual exploitation to forced marriages of adolescent girls, the numbers are extremely high, with very few of the victims ever reaching out for professional help. Gender violence takes place all over the world, including bullying and body-shaming at school or amongst peers, with girls suffering more psychological bullying than boys. As for sexual harassment, it matters not if women hold notable positions within society are sit at the lower end of the social strata - all can be victims of sexual harassment. Social media has been cited as one of the main channels through which women experience violence of this nature, with many female users reporting receiving death, rape, assault, or abduction threats towards them or their families.

Sadly, the problem also remains across Latin America and the Caribbean, with the percentage of women reporting physical abuse by their partners ranging from 19 to more than 50% across twelve different countries. The Mirabal legacy may live on, but systemic violence against women is clearly still very common to this day. While state-orchestrated oppression might be frowned upon by the public at large, interpersonal violence is often ignored, covered up, or even seen as an 'acceptable' part of life for many.

The price of violence

Violence against women eats away at the very fabric of society with far-reaching effects. Physical and psychological wounds, death, as well as social and economic costs, have repercussions on everyone. When women and girls are prevented from fully participating in the wider economic and social life of a country, the fallout is enormous. In some countries, the economic cost is estimated at up to 3.7% of the GDP, making the countries a lot poorer because of lost contributions.

All dictatorial regimes work in the same way: they support those who are their allies and suppress others who speak out against them, regardless of age, gender, or occupation. Violence comes in many guises and is not always as obvious as a murder, but it embeds itself within the legislation, the policies, the workplace, and often within the public psyche itself. Just as the Mirabals did, we all have a duty to call it out, expose it, and oppose it in whatever way possible.

It takes courage, guts, and bravery to stand up to an authoritarian power, which is why it is so difficult to do. And yet, it is needed just as much today as it was 60 years ago on the tiny Caribbean island of the Dominican Republic.

CONCLUSION

"How does one become a butterfly?
You have to want to learn to fly so much that you
Are willing to give up being a caterpillar."
—Unknown

Violence against women is carried out within the same narrative in all countries: male privilege and the submission of women. Patriarchy or machismo may be more obvious in some cultures than others, but it continues to exist in a multitude of forms across the board. It can be prevented through legislative frameworks that seek to protect the rights of all citizens, although this ideal scenario doesn't exist everywhere. On the contrary, legislation may actually be implemented that clearly restricts womens' rights under the pretext of religious or cultural beliefs.

History shouldn't be erased as it's crucial in helping us to remember events that must not be repeated. Rather than succumbing to the 'cancel culture', the male obelisk that Trujillo built in honor of himself on the Malecón in Santo Domingo is a fitting example. The phallic structure once stood as a sign of the leader's potency and power but today has been repossessed in honor of the Mirabal sisters. The 137-foot structure was painted with 'A Song to Liberty' by artist Elsa Nuñez and unveiled on March 8, 1997 in celebration of International Women's Day.

In a way, the obelisk represents all that Trujillo stood for: megalomania, self-importance, and a larger-than-life persona. But it also reveals his very weakness: a thirst for power that drove him to do the unthinkable; to carry out a brutal murder that would eventually cause his own downfall. The towering structure reveals more about the strength of the Mirabal sisters than that of the dictator.

Perhaps he always knew that he was impotent in the face of the women who dared to speak out against him. After all, he must have realized from his very first encounter with Minerva that she wasn't afraid of him. Although it has been said that as a leader, Trujillo would have been too busy to concern himself with the particular political activities of the Mirabals, the facts tend to suggest otherwise. Their activities were very much a personal issue for him, which is why he arranged to have them viciously murdered and thrown off a cliff that fateful day.

His actions reveal the inner cowardice of a man who was desperate to retain power, but also those of a fool. Like many ruthless dictators, he did not understand that making his enemies martyrs was a big mistake. Despite being one of the most despotic, feared men of his time, he was eventually destroyed by three young women who had no intention of yielding to his iron will.

After Trujillo's downfall and the subsequent establishment of a fledgling democracy, many exiles returned home to their beloved island. They were eager to put the past behind them and look forward to a bright new future. As the years passed by, the Dominican Republic found relative stability, while its neighbor Haiti continued to be at the mercy of political inefficacy, natural disasters, and poverty. By burying the past, at least the Dominicans could move forward with the optimism that they would never suffer at the hands of dictatorship again.

But Trujillo's ghost still walks the backroads of the country, albeit this time under a new guise. As painful memories are erased over the years, lingering only in the minds of those old enough to remember El Jefe, it also provides the opportunity for new would-be sycophants to appear through the woodwork.

Almost sixty years after the dictatorship came to an end, Trujillo's grandson, Ramfis Domínguez-Trujillo, decided to pursue a political career in the Dominican Republic. After growing up in Miami, in 2016 Rufis declared his intentions to run for President of the Dominican Republic in the 2020 election. By late 2019, he had agreed to represent the National Citizen Will Party but was blocked by constitutional laws that forbid him to run because of his dual nationality.

His desire to pursue political power was controversial, especially his intentions to rule with a 'mano dura' — a hard hand — and promising to build a Trump-like wall along the border with neighboring Haiti. A problematic subject, many Haitians continue to pass in and out of the country as migrant labor and still face great discrimination and poverty.

In 2020, Ramfis also came under fire for allegedly pocketing over $5 million of US taxpayer's money through political activities such as dinners, lunches, and other fundraising activities to finance his presidential candidacy. All of this, knowing full well that he would never meet the requirements stipulated by the country's legislation concerning residency.

Supposing that Trujillo's grandson had been able to legitimately run for power, it is difficult to say how successful he would have been. Whether or not the collective memory of the Dominicans would be strong enough to prevent the horrors of the past from happening again is something we shall never know.

Today, the Dominican Republic is a popular tourist resort, famous for its powdery beaches, lush landscapes, luxurious resorts and colonial charm. Despite the influx of tourism, a report by the World Bank in June 2021 noted that, *"disparities in access to economic opportunities and public services remain deep."* Poverty is particularly high in rural areas, with women feeling the brunt of the economic crisis that has arisen recently. The COVID-19 pandemic caused the first recession in the country for 17 years, having a negative impact on poor households, women, and casual workers.

The people of the Dominican Republic have a history of loss, hardship, and inner turmoil, yet maintain a vibrant love for life. Anyone visiting the Caribbean island will find themselves immersed in a rich, welcoming culture that is proud of its heritage and natural beauty. There is no time for sorrow on the streets of Santo Domingo.

… … … … … … ….

The Mirabal family had lost a lot: their father, their property, their family security, but not their determination to fight for freedom.

They represent every woman who speaks out against injustice, every mother who wants a better life for her children, and every daughter or sister who seeks to live a life of peace.

The Mirabals are you and I; they are alive today, shouting on the streets of Brazil, making their voices heard in China, and fighting for equal rights in the US.

Trujillo knew that he couldn't silence the Mirabals by fair means, for their roar shook the very foundations of everything he stood for. While he will go down in history as one of the cruelest tyrants of the 20th century, the Mirabals will continue to be remembered for their unwavering dedication and bravery. Their name is now a world symbol of the struggle of women and the elimination of violence while their surviving sister, Dede, was the voice that kept their story alive.

There are millions of Minervas, Patrias, and Marie Teresas all over the world. Women and girls are suffering systemic violence, ingrained gender discrimination, social inequalities, and domestic abuse in every society.

Not all women are political activists. Some move within the shadows, walk alone, or find the inner strength to survive domestic or state violence every day.

Many are openly pulling down the walls of power brick by brick while others hear the inspiring stories of their sisters and feel empowered to take action. Women are rewriting the narrative and making their voices heard. They cannot and must not be silenced.

We can all transform the world around us.

We can all spread our wings and fly.

We are all butterflies.

AUTHOR'S NOTE

The Background

The United Nations has been actively campaigning against gender-based violence since the Convention of the Elimination of All Forms of Discrimination against Women (CEDAW) by the UN General Assembly in 1979. Despite that, violence against women and girls continues to exist on a global scale.

Resolution 48/104 by the General Assembly lay the foundation for a world free of gender-based violence.

In 2008, the initiative known as the UNiTE to End Violence against Women was established, with the aim of raising public awareness around the issue. It also sought to increase policymaking and resources dedicated to ending violence against women and girls worldwide.

To date, only 2 out of 3 countries have declared domestic violence to be illegal, while 37 countries worldwide still do not recognize rape as a criminal offense if it occurs within the context of a marriage and 49 countries currently have no laws protecting women from domestic violence.

A Day for the Elimination of Violence Against Women

November 25th has been recognized by activists as a day against gender-based violence since 1981, in honor of the Mirabal sisters.

On December 20th 1993, the General Assembly adopted the Declaration on the Elimination of Violence against Women through resolution 48/104.

Finally, on February 7th 2000, the General Assembly adopted resolution 54/134, officially designating November 25th as the International day for the Elimination of Violence Against Women. Every year on the same date, governments, international organizations, and NGOs are invited to join together and organize activities designed to raise public awareness of the issue.

For more information on the UN resolutions and to learn how you or your organization can become involved in activities to raise public awareness on the issue of violence against women, please go to the UN website.

www.un.org/en/observances/ending-violence-against-women-day

Hi there,

If you enjoyed reading this book, please go to my amazon page and leave a review. I will appreciate it greatly.

Thank you so much!

Zoe

ABOUT THE AUTHOR

Zoe Marquetti is from Lima, Perú. Her high school and college years were spent during a period of political turmoil and terrorism with the Shining Path. The population experienced low self-esteem and morale, even though the country was so rich in culture and resources. Society was changing. These events aroused Zoe's interest in history and sociology, leading her to go on to study and receive a major degree in Archeology. Her interest in history, especially the role of women in society throughout the years and across different cultures, inspired Zoe to write this book.

Zoe loves learning more about different cultures, something that she enjoys doing through her travels. She is also a passionate cook and an advocate in the fight against animal cruelty.

ACKNOWLEDGMENTS

This book has been written in honor of the protagonists of this story, Minerva, Patria, Maté, and Dedé. Their courage and strong belief in justice has been an inspiration. Their story is still relevant today with so many cases of violence against women around the world.

My deepest gratitude to my editor Wendi Jane Ellis. This book couldn't have been possible without her support. I'm thankful for her honesty and all her insights during so many video calls.

Finally, thank you to my husband Ricardo for your love and continued support in all my endeavors, particularly in the creation of this book.

SOURCES

http://casamuseohermanasmirabal.com/

https://dominicantoday.com/dr/local/2021/05/30/what-is-known-about-the-plan-that-ended-trujillo/

https://evaw-global-database.unwomen.org/en

https://worldpopulationreview.com/country-rankings/dictatorship-countries

https://www.academia.edu/1065186/Rank_Usurpation_of_Power_The_Role_of_Patriarchal_Religion_and_Culture_in_the_Subordination_of_Women_A

https://www.academia.edu/206747/The_Political_Memory_of_Earthquakes_During_the_Colonial_Period

https://www.academia.edu/28445522/Rewriting_the_Trujillato_Collective_Trauma_Alternative_History_and_the_Nature_of_Dictatorship

https://www.academia.edu/32164628/Disaster_and_the_New_Patria_Cyclone_San_Zen%C3%B3n_and_Trujillos_Rewriting_of_the_Dominican_Republic

https://www.academia.edu/33629345/Writing_from_memory_history_stories_and_narrative_voices_ln_The_Time_of_the_Butterflies_by_Julia_Alvarez

https://www.academia.edu/38024058/Feminist_Histories_of_the_Interwar_Caribbean_Anti_colonialism_Popular_Protest_and_the_Gendered_Struggle_for_Rights

https://www.amazon.com/Caribbean-Racisms-Connections-Complexities-Racialization/dp/1137287276

https://www.amazon.com/Falsificaron-Firma-Dios-Viriato-Sencion/dp/B01K3MRGJC

https://www.amazon.com/Farming-Bones-Edwidge-Danticat/dp/1616953497

https://www.amazon.com/fiesta-del-chivo-Spanish/dp/9681906993

https://www.amazon.com/Time-Butterflies-Julia-Alvarez/dp/1565129768

https://www.amazon.com/Trujillo-Little-Caesar-Caribbean-German/dp/1245549855

https://www.amazon.com/Vivas-jard%C3%ADn-Spanish-Dede-Mirabal/dp/0307474534

https://www.bbc.com/news/world-latin-america-13560512

https://www.cambridge.org/core/journals/americas/article/abs/intimate-violations-women-and-the-ajusticiamiento-of-dictator-rafael-trujillo-19441961/DA58CD9173EB3017F791E41B0F03899D

https://www.cambridge.org/gr/academic/subjects/politics-international-relations/comparative-politics/how-dictatorships-work-power-personalization-and-collapse?format=PB

https://www.hrw.org/asia/north-korea

https://www.islanegra.com/index.php?option=com_virtuemart&view=productdetails&virtuemart_product_id=176&virtuemart_category_id=11

https://www.smithsonianmag.com/travel/what-became-of-the-taino-73824867/

https://www.unwomen.org/en/what-we-do/ending-violence-against-women/facts-and-figures

https://www.worldbank.org/en/country/dominicanrepublic/overview#1